# The Witch Ball

## and other short stories

by

## Doreen Valiente

Published by The Doreen Valiente Foundation
in association with The Centre For Pagan Studies

# The Witch Ball
## and other short stories

## by Doreen Valiente

Copyright © 2017
The Doreen Valiente Foundation

Design & Layout: Sarah Kay

Editors: Julie Belham-Payne, Sarah Kay

Cover Artwork: Doreen Valiente

Printed by Lightning Source International

ISBN: 978-0992843090

Published by The Doreen Valiente Foundation
in association with The Centre For Pagan Studies

www.doreenvaliente.org
www.centre-for-pagan-studies.com

# About the Author

## The Magical Life of Doreen Valiente

Ronald Hutton, Professor of History at the University of Bristol, calls Doreen Valiente "… the greatest single female figure in the modern British history of witchcraft".

Born on 4th January 1922 in Colliers Wood, South London, she was aware from her youngest years that there were other dimensions of reality, telling of an "indescribably mystical experience" which she had one twilight aged nine.

A rather rebellious time at school led on to wartime employment at the code-breaking establishment of Bletchley Park.

Marrying Casimiro Valiente in 1944, Doreen moved to Bournemouth, where she began to tap into the considerable local interest in all aspects of the occult, including a well-stocked local library and Spiritualist and Theosophical groups. The fortuitous acquisition of some notebooks from the Order of the Golden Dawn set her on the path to magical practice, leading eventually to a meeting with prominent witch, Gerald Gardner.

Gardner had been initiated into a witch coven in the nearby New Forest and ran a museum of witchcraft.

Doreen was impressed and was initiated by Gardner in 1953. She co-operated with him on several ventures and was an active member of his coven.

Disagreements over publicity caused her to leave the coven in 1957, by which time she was living in Brighton, her home for the rest of her life.

Doreen wrote her first book, *Where Witchcraft Lives*, about witchcraft in Sussex, in 1962. As she developed her own distinctive approach, Doreen wrote a further four books, including her 'magnum opus', *Witchcraft for Tomorrow*.

These books have influenced many over the years, being sensible, inspiring and well-written. The publication of *The Charge of the Goddess*, a book of her poetry, in 2014, together with the present volume, are testament to her considerable writing skills.

Doreen died in 1999 at the age of 77.

Philip Heselton
Author of the biography *Doreen Valiente Witch*
June 2017

# Other books by Doreen Valiente

Where Witchcraft Lives

An ABC of Witchcraft

Natural Magic

Witchcraft for Tomorrow

The Rebirth of Witchcraft

Witchcraft: A Tradition Renewed (with Evan John Jones)

Charge of the Goddess

# Editor's Foreword

When my late husband, John Belham-Payne and I found the manuscripts for these delightful short stories among the collection that Doreen Valiente bequeathed to him we said that we must share them by publishing them.

Now, finally, due to the great team we have around the Doreen Valiente Foundation, we are realising that dream. On his behalf, and mine, I would like to thank most sincerely the following people for all their hard work, dedication and talent in developing this work and now presenting it for the first time, in a book for others to enjoy.

Thank you, Sarah Kay - layout artist, Debbie Lewis - illustrator, Melissa Harrington - proofreader, and Ronald Hutton - proofreader.

You will love Doreen's unmistakeable style, and become engrossed in the way she weaves layers of metaphor into each story and character - enjoy!

Julie Belham-Payne
Spain June 2017

# Introduction

This book is an exciting addition to the literature of Doreen Valiente. Posthumously published it represents a lost work by one of contemporary Paganism's most loved authors.

These short stories feature the area Doreen lived in and loved, the folklore and history she avidly researched, and the philosophy and magic of which she was a leading exponent.

The main protagonist is Charles Ashton. He is wise, kind and learned, with a deep knowledge of folklore and magic, quietly tutoring his younger friend Jeremy Blake. Everybody who was fortunate enough to spend time with Doreen will recognise these qualities in Doreen herself. John Belham-Payne, to whom she left her magical and literary estate, was inspired to publish her poetry and her short stories, and to preserve her legacy in trust; and this work continues in his and Doreen's memory.

These short stories are not only of significance to fans of Doreen Valiente, they are of import within the interesting genre of magical tales written by magical practitioners. Earlier notable authors include Dion Fortune, whose short stories cross over with early twentieth century psychoanalytical psychology, and whose novels *The Sea Priestess* and *Moon Magic* have contributed ritual material to many Wiccans' Books of Shadows, alongside the poetry and prose of Doreen and others. Aleister Crowley's fiction gives an insight into the mind of a magician in a way that non-fiction cannot. His novel *Moon Child* describes an Abbé of Thelema that is a blueprint rather than a record of his Abbé in Sicily, which is now a site of esoteric pilgrimage.

Doreen Valiente was something of an antithesis to Crowley, she never had time for followers, hierarchies or magical organisations. She was most interested in finding the elder magics of the ancient Gods, and the ways of the traditional witch, and she never gave up her search. These short stories are imbued with the witchy atmosphere of the places she travelled to, the myths and folklore she collected, as well as some of the magical knowledge she assiduously noted in her vast personal library, most of which remains unpublished.

However, the reach of this book goes beyond the magical community. Unlike the fiction of the above authors it is not an overt exposition of magical teachings, Doreen's non-fiction is replete with that. These enjoyable tales weave and layer magic and folklore into a notable contribution to the wider genre of gothic fiction and folk horror. Here the reader can savour Doreen's deft use of time-honoured motifs within these genres, and may directly compare her short stories to those of literary greats such as Sheridan le Fanu, H P Lovecraft, Arthur Machen, Algernon Blackwood, and Dennis Wheatley, with a nod to Anthony Shaffer along the way.

Even 18 years after Doreen Valiente's death she never ceases to amaze, and this milestone publication enthrals us with her contribution of magic, magicians, witches and folklore to mainstream literature, all conveying the sense of decency, adventure, scholarship and humour that typified this remarkable woman. It is with enormous gratitude from the international Pagan community that Julie Belham-Payne, and the trustees and volunteers of the Doreen Valiente Foundation, are fulfilling John's dream of bringing this book to life, and further preserving the remarkable legacy of "the Mother of Modern Witchcraft".

Melissa Harrington
Cumbria, 2017

# Contents

# Illustrations

All illustrations are by Debbie Lewis with the exception of the
drawing of Buxted church on page 55 by John Belham-Payne

# About Debbie Lewis

I was born in the West End of London and worked there for many moons as a freehand visualizer in advertising. Meanwhile I engaged in various arts including drawing and painting. I am currently a tattooist in our family studio within Havering, where I was adopted as a baby. I thank my family for their patience and love. A seeker of truth, I offer these drawings to thank the Mother of Modern Witchcraft, Doreen Valiente, for her generosity, wisdom, magical words and love of the craft; to support the vision of the late John Belham-Payne; and in gratitude to their loved ones and friends, and all our family of the Craft, in the quest for the safekeeping and future preservation of Doreen's magical artefacts by the DVF. May we honour and remember our ancestors and reclaim who we truly are.

Find out more about Debbie here:

www.avalonillustrations.co.uk

# The Witch Ball

"*Caveat emptor* - let the buyer beware. Yes," said the elderly gentleman, smiling over his cup of coffee, "the old Latin tag is a good phrase to remember, especially when buying antiques."

He and his companion were sitting in the lounge of a Brighton seafront hotel, watching the rain as it pattered on the big window, blowing from the horizon of a tumbling grey-green sea. There was no question of a walk on the front on this stormy day of changeable autumn. A fireside chat in a hotel which was old-fashioned in all the right ways was a much pleasanter idea.

The younger man, Jeremy Blake, was attending a business conference; but he had left the large and imposing establishment in which it was being held, in search of a quiet lunch in more peaceful surroundings. Hence he came to be sharing a table with the older man, Charles Ashton, who had temporarily left his country cottage for a few days by the sea in Brighton, visiting an antiques fair, shopping and looking up old friends.

The two men fell into conversation and Blake found that Ashton was a retired antiques dealer. He was evidently a man of wide knowledge. Moreover, he had a quiet charm of manner which made his discourse interesting.

After lunch, they had adjourned to the lounge for coffee. Blake remarked on what a great place for antique shops Brighton was; on bargains to be found; and on curious and wonderful discoveries to be made by those sufficiently sharp-eyed and well informed.

These remarks, in their turn, elicited from Ashton a number of stories, told quietly and with a discreet smile, about finds, fakes, frauds and things a young buyer should know. Then, after voicing the well-worn Latin phrase, the older man fell silent and reflective for a few moments, sipping his coffee and gazing into the fire.

Finally he said, "There is one other risk in my profession. A remote risk, admittedly; you may never come across it; you may indeed scoff at it; but I and others have encountered it."

"What risk is that?" Blake asked.

"The risk, you might say, of an object having too much history," Ashton replied.

"I don't quite follow you," said Blake.

"Then," said Ashton after a pause, "I will tell you a story. You may regard it as you wish. I can only say that it is true. Do you know what a witch-ball is?"

"Oh, yes," Blake responded. "They're those big shiny glass balls that you sometimes see hanging up in antiques shops. I remember years ago there used to be a huge silver one hanging in a dark little shop window in Brighton Lanes, with a quite life-like effigy of a witch on a broomstick. I used to be rather scared of it as a kid. It's gone now."

"Yes," said Ashton, "I remember it. People used to hang these witch-balls in the windows of their homes, you know. They were supposed to avert the power of the evil eye. And, in the occult, they had other uses."

"The occult?" queried Blake. "Do you believe in that? You know, I've always wondered if there was really anything in it. But the people I've met up to now who professed to be occultists - well, frankly, they haven't inspired much confidence."

"I not only believe in it," replied Ashton gravely, "I think that experiences of what people call the occult or the supernormal are much commoner than is generally supposed. But those who have experience of such things hesitate to talk about them for fear of being classed as fools or impostors. And so a whole area of human life gets hidden behind a curtain, so to speak. That is what the word 'occult' really means, you know - hidden.

But to return to the story I was telling you. It concerns a witch-ball - one that I once bought. I had a fancy to have a good specimen to hang in my shop-window as an ornament. So when I saw one at a country house sale, I purchased it. It was a fairly large one in silvered glass (they're the oldest kind, you know, the coloured ones came later), showing some signs of age but all the better for that, I thought.

Well, it was at the week-end, so I didn't take it into the shop but brought it up into my flat above. It was a dark, chilly winter evening; so I made myself some tea and set about cleaning and looking over the things I'd bought. In particular, I gave the witch-ball a good polish with a soft duster and made it shine more brightly, as it leaned against a pile of old books on my table in the half-dusk.

I sat down in my armchair for a rest, being thoroughly tired, and decided to pour myself another cup of tea before I bothered to get up and put the light on.

How that old witch-ball gleamed, I thought as I watched it; almost as if it had a light of its own, a curious greenish light. How its curved surface dimly reflected the contents of the room, distorting them into strange shapes, making the familiar into something unfamiliar, something else altogether. What indeed were the objects reflected in the ball, showing themselves in such spectral shapes? There was the window, there the book-case - or was that dark shape really my book-case?

There was my face - but it was *not* my face!

I found myself looking for a fearful moment into two quite unfamiliar eyes; into the pale, handsome face of a woman, a face surrounded by long, dark ringlets of hair, of the style favoured in the early nineteenth century. And believe me, it was a bad face, a face which burned inwardly with some hellish intent.

I sat perfectly still in my chair, frozen with fright and with a kind of hypnotism. I could not look away.

Then the face seemed to move back into the mirrored vision, so that I could see the whole scene. The figure it belonged to was that of a well-dressed lady in the costume of that period; dark-coloured silk or velvet it looked like, sewn with small glittering beads. She was standing beside a polished table in a room lit by candles and flickering fire-light. On the table were various cut-glass decanters and a silver tankard on a small tray.

The lady took up the tankard and very carefully and deliberately poured into it, or into whatever drink it contained, the contents of a little green glass bottle. The she stirred the tankard with a spoon and stood looking at it. I saw cold, cruel resolution in her face, tempered only with fearfulness of discovery.

For how long she stood and for how long I watched, I do not know. Then she moved and took up the tray with the tankard. She came closer, turning her face towards me. Then her full red lips slowly curved into such a fiendish smile that I could not bear the thought of meeting those eyes again.

I think I cried out aloud. At any rate, the empty teacup and saucer fell from my hands and crashed to the floor. The noise seemed to break the spell. Once again I was looking at my own room, with the curtains open and the dusk illuminated by the kindly glow of the street lamp outside, not the weird greenish witch-fire of that silver ball.

I dashed to the light-switch and filled the room with light; and then, I can assure you, I went in search of something stronger than tea! When I had calmed down a bit, I looked at the witch-ball again. It looked perfectly normal: and in fact, I never saw anything else strange in it. But I changed my mind about keeping it in the shop!

It would be nice to be able to round off this story as M. R. James used to do, by saying that I asked questions about the old country house the witch-ball came from and learnt of a mysterious murder by poison that took place there many years ago, or something like that. But in practice, you know, one can seldom find out much.

Oh, yes, the details of the lady's costume helped me by indicating the right period - early nineteenth century, as I said. But there wasn't much to go on, except that the estate had changed hands around that time. Apparently the squire died rather suddenly and his widow sold everything. His relatives kicked up a bit of a fuss and tried to contest the will; but they didn't get anywhere. Then in later years there were some vague stories of a haunting; and that's about all. Anyway, isn't there a poet who tells us that all houses in which people have lived and died are haunted houses?

I did learn one thing, though. In reading up on the history of these witch-balls, I found that one of the uses they were actually put to in witchcraft was to induce clairvoyance. The seer sat in a dim light just as I had done and watched the ball until the reflected scene in it changed and something else appeared. The clever scientific people would call it auto-hypnosis, I suppose. But I think I saw the face of a long-dead murderess at the very moment of her most evil resolve."

For a brief while the two men sat in silence, as the autumn rain dashed against the window and the fire crackled faintly on the hearth. Eventually Blake enquired,

"But what happened to the witch-ball?"

Ashton chuckled. "Well," he said, "I must confess, though I'm rather ashamed of it, that I sold it off as soon as I could, to a couple of wealthy show-business people whom I didn't like very much!"

Blake joined Ashton in a rather relieved laugh; but Ashton became suddenly serious again. "You know," he said, "It's a very queer coincidence about those people - the ones who bought the witch-ball, I mean. But not long afterwards, *he* was rushed to hospital with an overdose of drugs or something and *she* was questioned about it by the police! Fortunately he recovered and the police couldn't prove foul play; but the couple are divorced now."

"I wonder which one's got the witch-ball?" said Blake.

"An interesting question," said Ashton.

# Vampire Love

"My story", said Charles Ashton, "has a classic beginning. Indeed, you will find it in Shakespeare: 'There was a Wight dwelt by a churchyard.'"

His younger friend, Blake, smiled; but not with total incredulity. He knew Ashton's extensive experience of life, as well as his unusual antiquarian knowledge. Since their first meeting in a Brighton hotel, the two had formed a friendship, based upon a shared liking for investigating those curious byways and sometimes-dangerous paths, which come under the general name of the occult.

After an excellent dinner in Ashton's country cottage near Ditchling Common, the two men were seated by the big open fireplace. Ashton, a member of the older generation, preferred music and good conversation to television; and Jeremy Blake found Ashton's company a pleasant occasional change from that of many of his fellow young executives, who seemed to have no ideas beyond sex, sport and money-making. So he listened with anticipation to another of the retired antique dealer's tales, told as it was by a log fire to the accompaniment of the steady ticking of a fine old grandfather clock.

"This particular Wight", said Ashton, "was a young chap I used to know, just starting up in the antique business. He was well educated, not one of the roughs we call 'knocker boys' who go around trying to con and browbeat people into parting with their valuables; but he hadn't got himself much of a shop yet, just a lock-up affair in a back street. So he lived in a basement flat in an old house very close to one of the oldest churchyards in Brighton, where there were tombs going back to the seventeenth century.

He was not a superstitious man. Once the curtains of his little flat were drawn and the lamps lit, it was cosy enough; and with the general shortage of housing accommodation, he was glad to get it.

He was anxious to acquire more stock for his shop; so he put an advertisement in the local paper. Something on the lines of: 'Best prices paid for small antiques' and a box number - you know the sort of thing. Then he would make arrangements to see the people who replied and negotiate with them.

Well, one night as he was sitting in his flat and all was quiet, he heard footsteps coming down to his front door and then a knock. He was wary of opening his door to strangers, especially after dark, as he usually had some valuables on the premises; so he was in the habit of looking through the window to see who was there before he went to the door. He did so on this occasion as usual, and to his surprise saw a young woman outside, apparently in evening dress and wrapped in a long dark cloak.

He went to the door and opened it, asking what he could do for his visitor. A low, musical voice replied, "I have something for you. May I come in?"

He assumed she had called in connection with he advertisement; though he was puzzled as to how she had obtained his private address. However, he invited her inside and asked her to sit down.

She removed her hooded cloak of dark blue velvet, and revealed a long low-cut gown of cream-coloured satin, high-waisted in the Regency style. He was surprised to see that she also wore long white gloves, a formality seldom seen today. Antique gold earrings, set with small diamonds, adorned her ears; dark-haired and dark-eyed as she was, they became her well.

The lady herself was strangely fascinating rather than beautiful. She was pale, with large, lustrous eyes and an abundance of dark wavy hair. Intrigued as he was, my young friend's first reaction was one of slight repulsion, he knew not why. But when she looked full at him with those strange eyes and smiled, he was wholly conquered.

"This is what I have brought", she said. "I wish to have it valued." And she produced from a beaded satin bag that matched her gown a small package wrapped in tissue paper, which she handed to him.

He unwrapped it and found himself looking at one of the finest cabochon garnet brooches he had ever seen, of the true deep blood red, with an antique gold setting. It seemed to him suddenly that the polished stone was indeed a drop of blood. He felt cold, and wondered at himself for so morbid a fancy.

He turned the brooch over in his hands; and then cried, "Ah, how sharp a pin it has! It has pricked me and drawn blood."

A bead of blood had appeared upon his hand, in that thick part of the palm which cheiromancers attribute to Venus. The lady's eyes brightened, almost flashed, as she saw it. Then, without further word or explanation, she gently clasped his injured hand and licked off the blood with her soft mouth.

Well, as you can imagine, that did for him. He was young, they were alone at night in a warm, softly lighted flat, the lady was seductive and willing, and all ideas of buying, selling and valuing flew clean out of his head. You can imagine what followed; I don't need to draw you a diagram."

Ashton seemed, at this point of his narrative, to become somewhat embarrassed. He rose from his chair to pour another glass of port. Blake smiled to himself, reflecting that Ashton was indeed one of the older generations. He accepted the refreshment of Ashton's good wine and the story was resumed, after the latter had gazed thoughtfully awhile into the red glow of the fire, an unusual sadness upon his face.

"Some hours later", said Ashton, "he awoke from sleep. To his surprise, he was alone. The lady had left as mysteriously as she had arrived. It was still quite dark. Putting on a warm dressing gown, he went outside and looked up and down the deserted street. Perhaps she had only just gone, he thought. Perhaps her exit had awakened him and he might see her hastening away. Surely he should escort her to her home? But no; there was nothing but silence, save for the distant cry of an owl in the churchyard trees and the light of a full moon silvering the old gravestones. He returned to his bed and slept heavily. In the morning, he wondered if it had really happened.

All he could recollect of her account of herself was that her name was Isobel Hartley and she was an actress; which would, he supposed, explain the late visit and the evening dress. Would he ever see her again, or would she regret a temporary madness? He felt strangely languid and unable to recollect the details of what had occurred. Suppose it had all really been a dream? But no, he had really punctured his hand somehow, for here were a few spots of blood upon the pillow.

The moon waned and the lady appeared no more. The young man's time passed in what seemed to him to be hopeless yet fascinated longing. It had been one of the strangest experiences of his life, yet he doubted if it would ever be repeated. Then, as the first quarter of the moon began to wax once more towards the full and he saw it shining through the branches of the churchyard trees, somehow he knew that he would see Isobel Hartley again. He even had a fancy that she was calling to him, especially when he lay at night in the borderline state between sleep and waking.

Then, on the night of the full moon, the light footfalls came down the steps once more. He hastened to the door, and there she was, dressed exactly as before, save that the blood-red garnet brooch was fastened at her bosom.

He tried absurdly to make some tongue-tied remarks, eager and utterly fascinated as he was to see her seated again in his flat by the light of a shaded lamp. He said something to the effect that he had not been able to value her brooch because she had not left it with him. She smiled, a Mona Lisa smile of the lips only, which did not reveal her teeth. "My brooch is beyond price in this world", she said, and entwined him in her arms.

You may have heard of love as partaking of the pleasures of heaven. Can you envisage a love which partakes of the pleasures of hell? For such was the love he experienced that night. Once again, there was the intensity of feeling accompanied by the dim recollection of detail. He seemed to float into another world, a world of dark, shadowy vastness and strange echoes of unearthly sound; a world dimly peopled by the shapes of all the nightmares which have haunted man since the dawn of time, passing before him in fantastic carnival, smiling sinister and urging him to join their revels. There were lamiae, beautiful women with great bird's claws for feet, grinning goat-footed satyrs, all weird and nameless abominations such as Breughel or Hieronymous Bosch dared to depict on their terrible canvases, leaping and flying through unearthly and desolate landscapes such as men have imagined to exist upon unknown worlds.

He knew that this was an unknown world but of another kind, a dimension forbidden to everything sane and normal, that Avernus of the ancients to which descent is easy but winning forth again not so. He knew that its depths were uttermost darkness and peril of body and soul. Yet when he awoke again with the daylight, alone as before and knowing nothing save that he was drained of life itself and could scarcely walk, falling back upon the bed several times when he tried to rise; even then, all he could visualise was the face of Isobel, all he could feel was the longing to embrace her again and feel her teeth close in what seemed a gentle love-bite upon his neck.

He was, however, not as yet completely overwhelmed. In the days that followed this last meeting, he began to rationalise the whole thing in his mind until he convinced himself that he was ill and even possibly the prey of some hallucination. He consulted his doctor, a cheerful down-to-earth physician to whom he did not feel able to confide the whole story, simply saying that he felt weak and unwell and was suffering from strange dreams. The doctor examined him and gave a verdict of anemia, prescribing a tonic and plenty of fresh air, rest and good food and adding in his jolly way, "You're in bad shape for a young fellow your age - nearly bad enough to need a blood transfusion!"

The young man took the doctor's medicine and some at least of his advice and began to feel better; but in the depths of his mind the obsession retained its throne. He waited on the changes of the moon, even though he had begun to suspect what they brought.

He might have been lost indeed, save for the circumstance that some work was to be done in the old churchyard, to repair and preserve some of its crumbling monuments which were considered to be of historic importance. The vicar of the adjoining church was a friend of our young man's, sharing his antiquarian interests. Although elderly, he was broadminded and knowledgeable in unusual ways, being remarkably free from that bigotry and ignorance which some members of the clergy unfortunately display in their attitude towards all things occult. Indeed, it was rumoured that he had been a member of a genuine magical order derived from the famous Order of the Golden Dawn.

This cleric informed the young man of the intended work in the churchyard, knowing that he would be interested in anything concerned with the preservation of antiquities. "You must come and see what we're doing", the vicar said. "I'm sorry to hear you haven't been well. It might do you good to get out and talk to people. You must meet the chap in charge of the work, he's very knowledgeable about old Brighton. Among other things, we're going to open the vault of Isobel Hartley."

It seemed to the young man that the clergyman eyed him rather narrowly as he made this statement. For himself, he was momentarily startled almost to faintness at the mention of the name; but by a great effort he managed to retain his self-command. Coincidence! It had to be mere coincidence!

The vicar was continuing: "You know, it's beneath that fine Regency period monument in the shape of a draped urn. We have to repair the base of it; it's become rather unstable. We know there's a vault underneath, although there's no inscription on the monument itself so we'll probably have to move the whole thing and then replace it. I should be sorry to see such a perfect period piece fall into ruin. It's quite a landmark in the churchyard when I look out across it from my bedroom window, especially on a moonlight night."

"Isobel Hartley?" The young man could scarcely breathe the question, chilled as he now was with the certainty that something more lay behind the vicar's words. Just what had he seen from that window in the moonlight?

Still professedly unaware of the impression he was making, the vicar went cheerfully on: "Yes, Isobel Hartley the actress. She was quite a celebrity in her time, you know, though she died too young to be remembered in the same way as people like the great Sarah Siddons. She was the mistress of a titled nobleman of the day, who was distracted with grief at her loss and did not long survive her. He erected that monument. There were some remarkable stories about her fascination for men. One of them claimed that she was involved in black magic. There were some queer things went on here in the past, you know. Most of the raffish crowd who hung around the Prince Regent, especially in the early days when he was merely Prince of Wales, were just drunkards and libertines; but a few were something more sinister. There are whispers about a revival of the eighteenth-century Hellfire Club, with an inner circle which was seriously devoted to the black arts. Isobel Hartley was a member of it.

"Well, I mustn't keep you talking too long, you don't look at all well. But if you would like to join me when we open the vault, I'll try to get it done tomorrow, while the sun is shining. We'll let the workmen do the preliminary work in the morning; and then when they've gone to their lunch, I propose to enter the vault."

The vicar took his departure, leaving the young man in a state of anxiety which he tried in vain to rationalise. He scarcely slept, pacing his room and awaiting the time when he would see either a wretched and frightening coincidence of names or - what?

Eventually the appointed time arrived. It was a bright sunny morning when the young man joined the vicar in the church porch to await the hour of noon when the workmen took their leave. As soon as they saw the men depart, they went across to where Isobel Hartley's monument had been displaced, disclosing a short flight of steps leading to a small underground vault. A heavy old-fashioned door secured it, with an equally heavy and antiquated iron lock; but the years had done their work on both and they presented little resistance to the vicar's crow-bar.

He flung the door wide and the two men stood back to permit fresh air to fill the dismal interior. Such was the position of the door that when it was fully opened the midday sun shone straight into the vault, which was the reason why the vicar, who as we have said was a knowledgeable man, had chosen this particular time to make his inspection.

The sun's rays disclosed a large coffin in the centre of the vault. With painful anxiety the young man craned forward. He saw a polished metal plate with the name: ISOBEL HARTLEY. The vicar, stern-faced and working silently and swiftly, proceeded without more ado to remove the coffin-lid. He placed the lid to one side, parted the folds of a silken shroud and beckoned the young man to look.

Then the silence of the vault was broken by an agonised cry; for the young man recognised only too well what lay within. There in her satin gown and all her strange beauty lay his love as if she were asleep; a beauty marred only by one small, abominable detail. Very slightly protruding between her lips were two pointed teeth.

The young man flung himself on his knees beside the coffin as if to embrace that life-like body; but even as he did so, the noonday sun shining upon it began to work a terrible change. The cheeks fell in, the colour faded from the lips -"

Ashton paused in his narrative as if unable to continue. For a moment he buried his face in his hands. Blake, who had listened to this tale in silent amazement, felt as if a cold air had invaded the room. The fire had burned low and there was no sound, save for the ticking of the ancient clock. Then Ashton sighed deeply, rose from his chair and replenished the dying fire with logs that sent a shower of sparks flying upwards. He resumed his seat and his story, speaking now quite calmly:

"In a few minutes it was all over. Before that young man's eyes, the body of Isobel Hartley fell first into corruption and then into dust, until there was nothing left within the coffin except a skeleton clad in the rotting remains of a satin evening dress. Upon its breast gleamed a brooch of cabochon garnet set in gold. The last thing the young man saw before he lost consciousness was the sunlight shining upon the red stone so that it looked like a drop of blood.

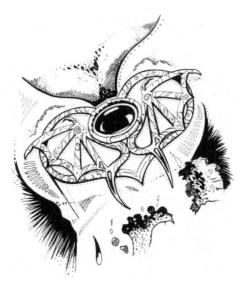

When he regained his senses, he was lying on the floor of the church vestry with his head on someone's rolled-up coat, while the vicar knelt beside him with a bottle of smelling-salts. The vicar spoke to him kindly and mercifully asked for no explanations, which on later reflection convinced him further that the rather unorthodox cleric knew a good deal more than he had said. As soon as his patient could be left, the vicar returned to the vault and made everything as secure and normal in appearance as possible. To anyone who had seen him helping the young man into the vestry, he explained that his friend was just recovering from an illness and the foul air from the vault had been too much for him."

"And the young man?" asked Blake as Ashton paused. "Did he recover? Did he ever see - *her* again?"

The clock struck its melodious chime, reminding both men that the hour was late. Ashton gazed into the fire with an expression which seemed at once enigmatic and sad.

"No", he said. "He never saw her again. And although he knew that the vicar had saved him from death and perhaps worse that death (for there are worse things), he almost hated him for doing so. But yes, you can say that eventually he recovered. Look here, Blake, you'd better sleep in the guest room tonight, it's much too late to go home."

Blake agreed and when the two men parted for the night he had asked his host no further questions about his strange tale. For looking at Ashton's face at the end of it, as he gazed into the firelight, Blake had received a sudden intuition as to the identity of the young man.

# The Cottage In Thorny Lane

"This isn't really my story", said Charles Ashton. "It was just told to me by a neighbour of mine. But you could say that it prompted me to a little research of my own."

He and his friend Jeremy Blake were enjoying a fine spring day's walk across Ditchling Common. They had been cheered by the appearance of opening buds, blue skies and the indefinable sense of stirring life borne upon the breeze; every year's perennial miracle. The unexpected warmth of the day had encouraged them to sit down for a rest in the sun; when Blake had taken the opportunity to ask if his friend had any new tales to tell from investigations into local folklore and odd happenings.

"Well", said Ashton, "We'll call the neighbour in question Mrs. Brown, although that isn't her name; and the young couple whom the story concerns I'll refer to as Bill and Sheila. They came to live in a small village near here, where they didn't really fit in. They were "townies", as the country phrase calls it.

Inevitably, Bill got bored and spent most of his evenings in the local pub. Not that I've got anything against pubs, in fact I like a drink in a good old-fashioned pub myself. But I don't believe in making the pub one's second home, especially at the expense of one's first home.

Bill, however, was one of those men who regarded it as natural that he should do as he liked and the wife should do as she was told. He usually referred to her as 'the wife', as one would refer the 'the cat' or 'the sofa' or any similar domestic animal or article of furniture.

Sheila was a nice little plain, downtrodden thing, neat and quiet. I think she had a strain of Celtic blood in her, hence the name which I have chosen to give her. She seemed to accept her lot, waiting dutifully on her husband and staying at home while he enjoyed himself with his friends. On a few rare occasions, she would go out, alone of course, to some little village function, a concert in the parish hall or some such thing.

One day, chattering to my neighbour, who was one of her few friends, she became for a while unusually bright and talkative. It seems that she had been returning from one of these little village get-togethers, and had walked home in the summer twilight down Thorny Lane, a rambling little road with big hawthorn hedges on either side of it. There, she said, she had found a charming old thatched cottage, occupied by a friendly old lady who had spoken to her and invited her in. She had paused to enjoy the sweet scent of the garden, full of old-fashioned flowers and aromatic herbs. Then first a large and portly black cat had come stalking down the path towards her, followed by the mistress of the house, who seemed pleased at Sheila's evident admiration. Soon, Sheila had been persuaded to enter the old lady's kitchen and have some of her homemade wine, which apparently was really remarkable, being blended with herbs and mead until it was almost a liqueur and served with little home-baked biscuits in the shape of crescent moons. Sheila had stroked the big black cat who stared at her with his jewel-like green eyes, admired the bygone kitchen implements that adorned the walls and left with a promise to call on the old lady again.

Mrs. Brown was glad to hear that Sheila had found a new friend. It would be good for the poor girl to have somewhere like that to go. Only one thing puzzled her. She simply could not recollect any such cottage being in Thorny Lane. Mrs. Brown had lived in the vicinity for some years and thought she knew it well. She finally came to the conclusion that Sheila must have got the name of the lane wrong. There was nothing in Thorny Lane except the long-ruined foundations of a cottage; and that was a place of ill-omen where, so local legend whispered, an old woman had once lived who was reputed to be a witch.

However, Sheila soon became a regular visitor to the cottage, in the evenings after Bill had gone to the pub. At first, Bill took little notice. He wasn't interested in old cottages or old women. But then he began to realise that Sheila was changing. She was becoming more self-confident, more independent; but not more talkative. She had always been quiet; now she seemed reserved, as if she had an inner life of her own, over which he had no power. In his loutish way, he resented this.

Matters came to a head when on the night of a full moon Sheila stayed out until long past midnight. Such a thing had never happened before on Sheila's side of the marriage, though it was by no means unknown on Bill's. Moreover, when Sheila finally did return to Bill's foul-mouthed rage, all she had to say was that she had been to old Mrs. Temple's cottage (for such apparently was the old lady's name) and she had only been away for a short while. Indeed, she seemed for a moment genuinely startled to see the time by the clock; but she soon recovered her composure and cut short Bill's bullying by drawing herself up, looking him straight in the eyes and calmly telling him to go to hell!

Such behaviour from a usually timid person like Sheila so amazed Bill that she had retired to bed before he could think of any reply. So the couple subsided into an uneasy truce; but trouble soon flared up again.

When the summer advanced into June, Sheila told Bill that she was going to spend Midsummer Eve at Old Mother Temple's cottage. Bill flew into another rage and proceeded to assert what he regarded as the rights of holy wedlock. He battered her to the floor with his fists, flung her into the bedroom, locked her in and went off to the pub. When he returned, he found the house in darkness. Sheila was lying on the bed, cold and stiff, in some sort of deep trance from which he was unable to rouse her.

Bill got thoroughly frightened, not for his wife but for himself. There were bloodstains and bruises that he was going to have to explain. He ran to Mrs. Brown and asked her to stay with Sheila while he fetched the doctor; which is how Mrs. Brown learned the foregoing details. Bill blurted them out in panic-stricken self-justification.

It took a while for the doctor to be found. However, by the time he arrived, Sheila was sitting up, apparently quite all right apart from cuts and bruises, and smiling as if at some secret joke. The doctor had a few stern words to say to Bill and that was that. But Mrs. Brown was puzzled by the peculiar trance-like state she had found Sheila in, especially as Bill insisted that Sheila had not been either unconscious or lying on the bed when he left her. Sheila had been so different lately. Was this going into trance something Old Mother Temple had taught her?

Once again, things subsided into apparent peace. Sheila said no more about Midsummer Eve; but Bill began to sleep earlier and more heavily than usual. Mrs. Brown's husband, who had an occasional drink in the same pub that Bill frequented, heard Bill telling his cronies that he believed Sheila was giving him something to produce this drowsiness; but he couldn't say how she was doing it and the other fellows only laughed at this.

Mrs. Brown was secretly piqued with curiosity to see whether Sheila would succeed in getting her way about spending Midsummer Eve with Old Mother Temple. She decided to keep watch unobtrusively and try to find out. Accordingly, she just happened, as she said, to be in the vicinity of the beginning of Thorny Lane as twilight fell on Midsummer Eve. She was still not sure just where the cottage was; but it must be round here somewhere.

It had been a perfect summer's day and the air was warm and still, full of the perfumes of grasses and flowers until it was almost sultry. The birds twittered to each other as they settled down for the night; soon there would be quiet except for the owls calling. The darkness thickened as the last red flares of sunset faded in the west. She was startled by the high-pitched squeak of a bat as it fluttered overhead. She had just begun to think of turning round for home when she saw someone going towards Thorny Lane. The person passed her swiftly and soundlessly. Was it Sheila?

She could not be sure, so she followed at a careful distance, until she was actually between the high hawthorn hedges of Thorny Lane. The woman in front of her looked like Sheila;

but what was she wearing? Mrs. Brown described it as a long trailing grey gown or cloak. The figure seemed to be gliding along rather than walking, going now more slowly, 'like a ghost' as Mrs. Brown put it.

It was almost dark now between the hawthorn hedges. Mrs. Brown realised that she could see the figure in front because it was surrounded by a faint light of its own. She began to feel very uncomfortable. She was sure the person in front was Sheila; but there was something strange about her. There was something strange and uncanny about the whole scene. There seemed, she said, to be a kind of tension in the air, a queer feeling of unreality. Ahead of Sheila was complete darkness; then in the distance appeared a reddish glow, as if from a bonfire. She heard sounds, shrill cries which seemed to be coming from a very long way off. Suddenly, the night seemed full of shadowy presences. Panic fright took possession of her. "I can't explain it", she said afterwards. "But everything seemed so eerie, I just turned around and ran. I never stopped till I was nearly home."

Now, Mrs. Brown is a stolid country woman, not one to take fright at the squeak of a bat or the darkling twilight of an unlit lane; so when she told me that she experienced something uncanny that night, I believed her. It upset her so much that she avoided Sheila for some weeks. Then, to her surprise, one day Sheila called in to see her. She told Mrs. Brown quite calmly that she was leaving Bill, because she was going to have a child that was not his. She wanted to say goodbye to Mrs. Brown, she said, because she had been one of her few friends.

Mrs. Brown was completely astonished. She even wondered if the story were true, because Sheila showed no obvious signs of pregnancy and didn't seem in the least 'that sort of girl', as she put it. She said goodbye to Sheila reluctantly, adding that she hoped she would be all right and asking if she had somewhere to go.

Sheila replied with a smile. "Yes," she said, she had somewhere to go. It was quite close at hand; but Bill would never find her.

"Is your child's father going to look after you?" asked Mrs. Brown. "Yes", Sheila replied. "I shall cross over and be with him for ever."

Puzzled by this enigmatic remark, Mrs. Brown felt tempted to refer to her strange experiences on Midsummer Eve; but somehow she felt unable to speak of it.

The next day Sheila disappeared. Bill came home from work to find a brief note saying that she had left him and was not coming back. Bill was furious. In the pub that night, he loudly blamed Old Mother Temple for his wife's defection and expressed his intention of going round to have it out with the old hag and make her tell him where Sheila was.

Mrs. Brown's husband was there and heard this. He knew of Sheila's conversation with his wife the day before, but kept his own counsel about it. He noticed, however, that at the mention of Old Mother Temple's name, two of the village grandfathers who were quietly playing dominoes at the back of the room looked up and then significantly at each other. Eventually one of them spoke: "Best not seek after Old Mother Temple." He might have said more but Bill downed his drink and swore that, old woman or not, he would have it out of her if he had to choke her. Then he strode out into the night and the old men resumed their silent game.

The next day, Bill did not arrive at work. His employer sent to look for him, but he was not at home either. Remembering the conversation of the night before, his friends organised a search party before darkness fell again. When they eventually found Bill, he was cowering, clean out of his mind, in the ruined foundations of an old cottage in Thorny Lane, where no one had lived for over two hundred years.

Whatever had happened to him that night had literally scared him out of his wits. There was nothing to be done but to take him off to a mental hospital, where he stayed for over a month. When he returned to the village, it was only to sell up his home before leaving for good.

Then one day, about three years later, Mrs. Brown saw Sheila again. The story of her disappearance and what had happened to her husband had been almost forgotten. Even Mrs. Brown's strange experience in Thorny Lane had faded into the back of her mind, so that she was not unwilling to go down the lane in daylight. On this summer's evening, however she was later than usual and twilight was beginning to gather. Suddenly, there before her was Sheila. Mrs. Brown described her as being 'oddly dressed in green - a long green dress with some sort of embroidery on it. And she had a little elvish boy with her.' Something about the two figures in the dusky lane seemed very strange to Mrs. Brown; but she seemed unable to describe what it was, except that for a moment she had experienced again something of that sense of unreality and gathering terror she had known on that past Midsummer Eve.

However, Sheila had smiled at her, as did the little boy peeping at her from behind his mother's skirts, a little bright-eyed, brown-faced rascal who seemed to be wearing very few clothes at all and to have curiously pointed ears. Sheila, indeed, looked well and happy; but when Mrs. Brown tried to approach nearer and speak with her she waved her hand as if in farewell. Then she and the little boy, hand in hand, went on round a bend in the lane. Mrs. Brown followed them. When she got to the bend, they both disappeared. As I told you, there were high hawthorn hedges on either side of the lane, so there seemed to be nowhere they could have gone to and Mrs. Brown realised there was no opening they could have come from either. Suddenly they had just been there. She was not so frightened as she had been before; but the twilight was darkening and she hurried home. She felt that she had touched the fringes of something unearthly; which is why she told the story to me. Knowing my interest in the occult, she wondered if I could offer any explanation of it."

"And could you?", asked Blake.

"Well", said Ashton, "if this tale had been told, say, a hundred years ago in the remoter parts of Ireland or Scotland, or even in certain districts of Wales, there is one explanation which would certainly have been advanced. That is, that Sheila had been taken by the fairies."

"Oh, come now!" Blake protested; but Ashton continued quite gravely.

"I don't mean the fairies of pantomimes and children's books. I mean the fairies that people *really* believed in: a race of beings with whom, usually invisibly, we share this earth. A race, moreover, who were called the Good Folk or the People of Peace for the same reason that the Ancient Greeks called the Furies "the Good Ladies": because ordinary mortals were afraid of them.

I've a curious old book at home in my library that you must see some time. It's called The Secret Commonwealth of Elves, Fauns and Fairies, by the Rev. Robert Kirk , M.A., who was the minister of Aberfoyle in Scotland. His book is dated A.D. 1691; but Andrew Lang's edition of 1893 is the one I have. The author died, or perhaps we should say disappeared, in very queer circumstances the year after the book was written; but that's another story.

Kirk describes the fairies as being 'of a middle nature betwixt Man and Angel, as were Daemons thought to be of old.' He mentions their 'light changeable Bodies (like those called Astral)' and says they are 'best seen in twilight.' But you must read the book for yourself. Another thing you will find in it is that the world of Faerie was closely associated with the world of witchcraft, as many of the records of witch trials will confirm. There are, too, a great many stories of human beings who were somehow enabled to find their way into this other world, or other dimension as we should call it today; sometimes merely for a visit and sometimes for ever."

"Old Celtic legends, yes," replied Blake. "But in Sussex today? The home of commuting stockbrokers? One hour by train from London?".

"Ah, yes; they call it seely Sussex", said Ashton. "Do you know what that means? It's from the Anglo-Saxon and means 'holy Sussex'; but it can't mean it in a Christian sense, because Sussex was actually the last English county to become Christian. It's full of the old paganism, if you get just a little off the beaten track."

"But the child?"queried Blake. "Surely that is impossible?"

"Who are we to say what is possible and what is not?"Ashton answered. "Our life is surrounded by mysteries, if we pause to think of it, which we seldom do. There are, however, a few facts in this case which my own investigation was able to establish. It seems that Thorny Lane is not the old name of that place at all. Years ago it used to be called Horney's Lane - not named after its hawthorn hedges but after Old Hornie, the horned god of the witches! The ruined cottage there was once occupied by a reputed witch. Her name was Agnes Temple. And there was a wood near the cottage which was said to be the meeting place for the witches' Sabbats. There's not much of it left now; but we'll have a walk down there one day, if you like."

"I'm not at all sure that I want to", said Blake. "Suppose it is really what you've been hinting at - one of those places which is a gateway into another plane of existence?"

"You will find that it looks a perfectly normal English lane", Ashton assured him. "By daylight", said Ashton,

"By daylight?" said Blake.

"By daylight" said Ashton.

# The Talisman Of The Moon

The two friends, Charles Ashton and Jeremy Blake, were talking by the fireside in Ashton's country cottage, as was their quiet and pleasurable pastime. As usual, the older man Ashton reminisced about the world of antiques, as he knew it from long experience, and about bygone days generally. Blake, who was interested in the preservation of the knowledge of the past, listened attentively, conscious of the privilege of knowing an antiquary like Ashton, who was a mine of out-of-the way information of all kinds; and so the talk drifted around to archaeology.

"Of course," said Ashton, "archaeologists are prosy, conservative sort of chaps usually; outwardly unimaginative at any rate. Which is perhaps just as well, when you consider the strange things they have to handle sometimes. Even so, many of them have had experiences which have never found their way into published books. I heard a very curious tale once, from a chap I used to go to school with. I don't imagine he would have told it to anyone but me.

I won't give you his real name, because he's become quite well-known now as a writer and broadcaster, so we'll call him Colin. At the time when the events of this story took place, he was a young chap just setting out in his career as an archaeologist, and he'd got a job helping with some excavations in Somerset, not far from the famous landmark of Glastonbury Tor.

I don't know if you are acquainted with the Glastonbury area at all; but it's a place full of strange tales of dreams and visions, legends and hauntings. The famous occultist Dion Fortune used to live there and wrote about its traditions; but that's another story. My friend Colin wouldn't have paid much attention to occultists and their beliefs at the time I am referring to. He was a determined humanist and skeptic, with no predisposition towards psychic experiences.

Well, in the course of his excavations at the site of this ancient British village that he and his colleagues from a certain university were studying, Colin himself unearthed a notable find. This was a fine bronze pendant, evidently some sort of amulet or talisman.

The pendant was in the shape of a crescent moon, with the horns pointing downwards and a ring on the upper edge by means of which it could be hung around one's neck. The design is frequently met with from Roman and pre-Roman days; indeed, it survives to this day as a popular shape for horse-brasses which, by the way, originated as amulets. It is evidently related to the moon and to ancient beliefs in its influence, which is very important in relation to ancient religions and also to magic and witchcraft.

This particular example, however, had something which made it different from others of its kind. On the back of the pendant was a row of sigils or magical signs. At least, that was what Colin concluded them to be; though he suspected that they might be letters of some archaic alphabet. At any rate there were nine of them, in three groups of three.

Colin was much intrigued by these mysterious signs. That night he took the talisman of the moon, as he had begun to call it, back to his hotel room in the little country town of Glastonbury where he was staying, because he wanted to try to decipher the sigils. In this, however, he had no success, and eventually he fell asleep with the gentle chimes of Glastonbury's church clock striking a late hour, and with the pendant lying on the table beside his bed.

He drifted into the world of dreams and found himself wandering in a strange country. He saw a flat, bare moonlit landscape where the sky was a deep purplish colour, so that he did not know if it was night there or day. The approach to this place was along an avenue of dusky trees, down which he found himself walking. Here and there were streams of water bordered by willow trees, whose leaves gleamed silvery through the dusk. Grazing beside one of the streams was a unicorn, which in the odd way of dreams seemed quite natural. In the distance was a ring of nine monoliths, set upon a hill.

Then he saw an indistinct crowd of dark-robed people coming towards him from the direction of this ring of stones. A sense of fright and foreboding began to oppress him but he could by no means escape what was coming. The shadowy figures came closer. At the head of them was an old bearded man, robed like the portraits of ancient Druids and of commanding presence. Beside him was a veiled figure which seemed to Colin to be that of a slim and beautiful young girl; yet Colin did not know which of them he was most afraid of.

The old man, with a menacing look, pointed at Colin's chest. Looking down, Colin saw that he himself was wearing the talisman of the moon, suspended around his neck on a string. He felt that he was somehow being accused – of theft, sacrilege, or what?

Indefinably alarmed, he turned to run. The black-clad people were close behind him. They were fanning out to encircle him! Out of the corner of his eye, he saw his pursuers melting from one form into another, but always close upon him; transformed now into black, furious hell-hounds, now into loping monstrosities and bat-winged, clutching shapes such as terrified the hearers of ancestral legends whispered around bygone hearth-fires. He ran with the awful slowness of nightmare, as if through water; and awoke with a muffled scream just as one of the black talons behind him seemed to grip his shoulder. He was bathed in sweat and conscious that it was the darkest part of the night and a long wait for dawn.

Eventually, as the first light filtered through the curtains of his bedroom, he fell again into an uneasy sleep. The nightmare had been unpleasantly realistic. But the day that followed was sunny and cheerful and the shadows of the night were soon banished from his mind.

He had an appointment that evening to visit some friends at a nearby village. He knew that they would be interested to hear of the progress of his archaeological 'dig'; so when he drove out to their home he carried the talisman of the moon with him, glad of the opportunity to display so interesting a find. The memory of his nightmare was already fading and dismissed as of no importance, just a psychological oddity.

Nevertheless, it was with some puzzlement and for a moment a little perturbation that Colin viewed the road to his friends' home, which he had not travelled before. Once outside the streets of Glastonbury, he found himself in the low-lying countryside of green meadows traversed by small streams which in olden times was much prone to flooding, hence the old name of the Tor and its surroundings as they rose above the waters: the Isle of Avalon.

Naturally, there was an abundance of willow trees here, with their affinity for streams. There was not really anything uncanny, Colin told himself, in the fact that he was now travelling along a narrow lonely road bordered on either side by such trees, and with a stream running beside it which made it wise to drive cautiously. It certainly resembled the country of his dream; but by the light of a pleasant, sunlit day there was nothing sinister about it. No unicorns, for instance, he told himself. No black pursuing shapes, either; funny what one's subconscious will conjure up. And he drove cheerfully on.

He spent a pleasant evening with his friends, whom he had not seen for some time before they moved to this place near Glastonbury. They showed him over the new home, which he duly admired. He enjoyed a good dinner and a glass of wine. Then he in turn talked about his work and proudly displayed the bronze talisman.

They agreed that it was a splendid find; but the lady of the house, whom Colin had sometimes joked with about her being psychic, didn't seem to like the talisman very much. When she held it in her hand, she said, it made her shiver. Had it, she asked, come out of a grave?

"No," Colin replied cheerfully, "you're wrong there. It was just buried in the centre of a mound. Rather unusual, that; as if it had been buried there deliberately for some purpose. The mound wasn't a barrow - you know, a burial place. More like a place of ritual."

As he spoke, a sudden recollection crossed his mind. The mound that he had seen in his dream! That sinister mound, topped with its ring of stones, from which had come the shadowy shapes of terror! It had been higher in the dream than the actual mound in which he had dug; but that would be the effect of erosion. And of course, the stones might have been there once and been carried away; so many stone monuments had been destroyed in the course of centuries. But no, he must stop such imaginings, this was nonsense, he told himself firmly. And he smiled at the psychic lady's assertion that such places had a duplicate of themselves upon the astral plane, which could persist through the centuries; even when she told him the strange but true story of the woman who had visited Avebury one summer evening and found herself travelling along an avenue of stones which in broad daylight were definitely no longer there.

They changed the subject and talked of books and the theatre and good old days at the university; so it was in no morbid frame of mind that Colin, warmed with his friends hospitality, set off again to drive back to Glastonbury.

By now it was almost dark; but the moon was rising and spreading a diffused, luminous moon-mist over the countryside. Negotiating the narrow, unlit road beside the stream and the willow trees was not easy. He had to drive slowly; but how beautiful and peaceful the scene was! The spreading Somerset meadows under the moon, with just enough light to make out here and there the remains of barrows and earthworks of long vanished races; the faint trickle of water in the stream, the soft soughing of air through the branches of the willows. Why hurry, he thought; why not stop a few minutes and enjoy the peace of this rare place, this Avalon of the Arthurian legends, this Ynys Wytryn of the still older pagan lore, in which Glastonbury Tor was the dwelling-place of Gwyn ap Nudd, the dread Lord of Annwn, the Celtic Otherworld.

Colin stopped his car and got out to look across the meadows, trying to discern the shape of the great Tor in the distance. A thicker mist was rising, white and ghostly, from the stream. The air grew suddenly chill, a deathly cold. He felt paralysed, unable to move. There was a sight he felt somehow destined to see; and it was coming towards him.

Slowly the mists parted and a boat of ancient shape came gliding towards him upon the stream. It moved in silence, or else he was in a state that could not perceive sound. Within the boat were two people: the veiled young girl and the old bearded man of his dream. Upon a breath of cold air they passed him by. As they did so, the old man raised his hand and again pointed accusingly at him. Then they vanished into swirls of mist and Colin realised that what he had seen was a vision.

How long he had been standing there motionless he did not know. He was chilled to the bone and profoundly shaken; for as I have said, he was a determined and professed skeptic, and such experiences are more shocking to people of that turn of mind than they are to believers in psychic or occult matters. That may sound paradoxical, but I have often observed it to be so.

Eventually, however, he pulled himself together sufficiently to drive his car on to Glastonbury. He returned to his hotel room and spent a very poor night; because, as he candidly admitted, he was at first afraid to sleep for fear of what dreams might bring. However, after the first light of dawn he managed to sleep a little; but when he returned to his work at the site the next day he was looking and feeling so haggard that his colleagues jokingly enquired what he had been doing to give himself such a hangover.

By the end of the day's work he was in no mood for jokes. He was grouchy with everyone and furious with himself. Inwardly, he called himself every kind of a fool to be so put out by a nightmare, so influenced by the talk of a silly superstitious woman, so overcome by the atmosphere of a place that he, an educated man, had actually imagined that he had seen a vision!

No, he corrected himself; he had experienced a subjective hallucination. To be able to give his experience a scientific name seemed somehow comforting. He held on to the thought - hallucination. And he would do something about it. He would defy the supernatural. He would go back to the willow path by night, to that lonely road by the stream – only not right away, he would give himself a night to get over it. But tomorrow night, yes, he was resolved; and nothing would happen. And he would take the talisman of the moon with him, as that seemed somehow to be the focus of the manifestations, the trouble, the unease – whatever one could call it. Yes, he would carry it with him, as the last touch of defiance!

Already feeing better, he went back to his hotel, ate a good dinner and got a fairly good night's sleep. The next day, work proceeded normally. By nightfall, he felt quite calm and ready to exorcise this spirit of superstitious ancestral dread that had come out of some dark corner of his own subconscious mind. Then one day he would be able to look at this talisman of the moon reposing harmlessly, neatly ticketed, inside a glass case in a museum – and he would be able to laugh at all this.

The moon was now just past the full, but still giving a flood of silver light. Indeed, the night was clearer than that night of soft moon-mist he had found so disturbing. The shadows were more sharply defined. As he drove his car along the willow path the moonlight glittered here and there upon the stream and the sky above was full of stars.

He found the place at which, or approximately so, he judged the previous manifestation to have occurred. Stopping his car as before, he got out and stood resolutely beside an old willow-tree, the night air cold upon his face. In his pocket his fingers closed around the talisman. The night was very still.

He waited, listening to the soft night sounds, determined not to be startled. That movement was the tread of beasts in some nearby field. That splash was a water-rat or some such creature, just near his feet. That cry overhead on the wind was a night-flying bird. And that shifting of the shadows upon the stream – what was that? Surely there was among them some darker shape?

Colin stared at the moonlit water. There seemed to be something more substantial there, a black bulk gliding slowly towards him. He had a moment of sheer fright, followed quickly by almost laughing relief. It was a tree-root – nothing but a tree-root, fantastically shaped. Floating slowly downstream! Of course it was a tree-root – he moved to the very edge of the water to be sure of it.

He leaned forward as the black object came level with him. Then he let out a yell of the greatest terror he had ever known, as the thing reared at him, black, gigantic, smelling of earth and deep water, wetly tentacled. It towered over him, overwhelming him with a blackness beyond midnight and a smell indescribable of ancient decay. He was dragged into the water, struggling blindly and desperately for his life.

Whatever kind of creature it was seemed to have no settled form just a monstrous shape of blackness stretching long writhing arms to drag him down. Its very presence inspired him with such panic horror that he almost lost consciousness. Indeed, it might have fared badly with him if his frantic cries had not been heard in time. However, a wavering light appeared upon the path. It was the lamp of a bicycle, ridden by a countryman who arrived just in time to pull Colin out of the water. And another strange aspect of this strange story is that the countryman saw absolutely nothing but the willows and the stream by moonlight. Nothing, that is, except Colin struggling, screaming and drowning in about two feet of water.

Well, the country chap, who proved to be a local farm worker, got him out and took him to his cottage. He offered to call an ambulance; but Colin asked him to telephone his friends instead, the couple he had spent the evening with on the night of his previous experience. They came and collected him and his car and did all they could – gave him brandy, put him to bed and so on. But it was a while before he could talk about what happened. When he did, he only said that he leaned over to look at something in the stream and fell in. He felt somehow unable to say anything more.

When he was well enough to put on his dried clothes, he found that the talisman was gone. He supposed that in the struggle it had fallen into the stream and sunk into the mud at the bottom. Out of Somerset earth it had come, and back to Somerset earth it had returned. He was in no mood to go and look for it; so it may well be there still."

Ashton paused in his narrative. The fire had burned low and he got up from his chair to replenish it. As he had often done before, Blake watched the shower of sparks flying upwards from the fresh logs and wondered at the tale he had just heard.

"But what *was* it?" he enquired. "This monster that dragged him into the water, I mean?"

"Shall we have a glass of wine and some biscuits before we discuss that?" Ashton replied. He produced a crystal decanter of excellent port and a suitable accompaniment of biscuits upon an antique silver dish. When the two men were settled again by the fireside with their drinks, Blake renewed his question. Ashton answered slowly and thoughtfully.

"There are several possibilities. One is that the thing was an elemental – a non-human entity of which there are many kinds in occult lore, some harmless and others highly dangerous. Elliott O'Donnell, that indefatigable collector of ghost stories, had many tales of such phenomena. Mediaeval magicians associated elementals with the four elements of earth, air, fire and water. Within this broad classification, elementals may be of many orders. Water elementals, for instance, may range from the beautiful and seductive forms of the undine or the naiad to such horrors as nearly encompassed the end of young Colin."

"Why a water elemental?" asked Blake.

"I think," Ashton replied, "because of the connection with the moon, the ruler of water. Remember the talisman of the moon, which seemed to be the original cause of these manifestations. Remember, too, the place in which they occurred, beside the willow-trees. The willow is ruled astrologically by the moon; in Ancient Greece it was sacred to Hecate, the moon-goddess of witchcraft. In our own countryside, the witch's besom is traditionally made of an ash stake, birch twigs and willow binding; that is, the long flexible willow branches called osiers. The willow is a tree of moon-magic, which is a very potent thing in both its light and its dark aspects."

"Could the talisman of the moon have been connected with moon-magic?" asked Blake.

"I'm sure it was," Ashton said. "And also probably with moon worship. Colin was undoubtedly right when he believed it to have been buried purposely in a ritual mound. It may have been put there to consecrate the place to some moon-goddess of Ancient Britain. Such sites were given guardians. That is, a power was established there by ritual; and when the site was violated that force came automatically into operation, when and where the conditions were right for it to manifest."

"Even after all this time?" said Blake.

"How much do we really know about time?" replied Ashton.

"The influence may get slowly weaker over the years, perhaps. But Colin sought no further for that lost talisman; and I too would be content to leave it hidden where it lies."

Doreen Valiente

# The Legend Of The Grove

It was so mild and inviting a summer day that Ashton and Blake had ventured far from their usual walks across Ditchling Common. Instead, they had driven in Blake's car out on to the open road across Sussex, under the clear blue canopy of an almost cloudless sky.

They had brought with them suitable provisions for a good picnic meal and the day was theirs. The young leaves of early summer were of their purest green as the sunlight streamed through them. The blackthorn blossoms, which had lain like snow upon the hedges were fast vanishing. In their place as the delight of the country scene appeared the flowers of old gnarled apple and pear trees in the cottage gardens, and great laden boughs of almond and cherry blossom in those of the more modern houses. Woods were scented with bluebells and starred with golden celandines. Everywhere was ageless joy. One could do nothing else on such a day, given the chance, but make a holiday of it.

What tale Blake had told at his office in order to take the day off, Ashton prudently did not enquire. He reflected that all work and no play was not food even for young executives, and normally Blake was hard-working enough. Anyway, such fresh sun-warmed air as this was good for both of them.

So under Ashton's guidance the two men drove towards Chichester on a good main road, but turned off before they reached the cathedral city and began to thread the country lanes. Their destination was a tract of ancient forest, centuries old, now fortunately cared for as a nature reserve.

"There is something quite unique about this place," said Ashton. "I want you to see it, because it is really a place of mystery. I've seen it once before and it has a remarkable atmosphere. I have been trying to find out more about it. For one thing, no one really knows how the great trees in this valley came to be planted. They are evidently a grove and one story is that they are Druidic."

"Surely they are not old enough for that?" queried Blake.

"It is hard to say," Ashton replied. "We really know so little about the old pagan faiths of Britain. These actual trees are at least five hundred years old; they may be the successors of even older trees. We know from Greek and Roman writers that the Druids performed their worship in sacred groves. But so did the devotees of still older faiths of nature-worship. The old Celtic word for a sacred grove is *nemeton*, and versions of it appear in a number of place-names. But I mustn't bore you with my researches."

"You don't bore me," Blake assured him. "But which turning do we take now?" Ashton directed him, until eventually the car drew into a field, which had been provided as a small car-park for visitors. As it was a week-day, there were only a few other people there. A cuckoo called persistently from a nearby wood, and the surrounding fields were inhabited by ewes and their young lambs and cows with newly-born calves.

"This is as near as we can get by car," said Ashton. "We'll have something to eat here and then walk down that lane over there, through the heathland and on to the inner grove. I'm glad it's quiet here today; one has a chance to feel the spirit of the place."

The two men enjoyed their picnic lunch and then, after locking the car, took walking-sticks and set off upon the indicated route. They reached the boundaries of the nature reserve, where yellow butterflies danced before them over the sweet-scented turf and budding hawthorn and wild rose gave promise of further glories to come.

"I don't see your mysterious grove," said Blake.

"You will in a moment," Ashton replied. "See that tangle of trees and undergrowth over there? Well, follow this little path."

He led the way along a path as narrow and winding as the one Thomas the Rhymer in the old ballad called the road to Elfland. They passed within the shade of higher and older trees, where the sunlight was left behind and a chill fell upon them. Blake saw before him a complete contrast to the sunlit heath outside. It was like being in a natural cathedral. He realised that this indeed was the *nemeton*.

"But the trees!" he exclaimed. "I believe you now when you say that they are centuries old. What are they?"

"They are yews," replied Ashton. "The longest lived of all British trees and hence the type of immortality. For that reason you will have seen them planted in old churchyards."

"But never such monsters as these," Blake said as he gazed around him. The gnarled trunks, tremendous in girth, did indeed seem in the half-light to assume strange writhing shapes. Here a huge upreared arm, there the suggestion of a giant face; while the outspread branches, bowed to earth and with extensions going down from them into the ground, where like the arched backs and crouching limbs of dragons. So deep was the shade that no grass grew beneath the trees; but here and there a shaft of sunlight penetrated the gloom of the mighty branches above and illumined the dark green of their leaves as it slanted to earth.

"You are right, Ashton, there is something awesome about this place," Blake remarked as they proceeded further into the grove.

"It reminds me," said Ashton, "of that passage in a work by the Roman poet Lucan (*Pharsalia*, I think it's called), in which he describes a sacred grove of the Celts that used to exist near Massilia, or Marseilles as the name is today. He tells how even the priest of that place entered it with dread, lest he should encounter the dark divinities that haunted there. The leaves of the trees moved sometimes when there was no breeze blowing to stir them. Birds and beasts of the forest avoided the place. The fantastically shapen trunks of the trees served as the images of gods, before which the blood of sacrificial victims was offered. Strange lights and sounds were perceived there by those who dared to enter, as well they might have been if blood sacrifices were really offered there. Such things always attract elementals."

"This place seems very silent," Blake interrupted nervously. "I've heard hardly any bird song since we entered."

"That is not necessarily sinister," Ashton replied. "Birds are not attracted to yew trees because there are relatively few insects there for them. Hence yew woods are sometimes called "birdless groves." Perhaps Lucan's grove was one such, and popular superstition supplied the rest." He smiled reassuringly at Blake's unease.

"I find peace in this place now," Ashton continued, "Whatever may have happened here in the past. Let us sit down awhile, by that shaft of sunlight, where the fallen tree-trunk is - no, I see it is a mere branch, as big as the trunk of any other tree. But it affords a good seat to rest on. Perhaps if we sit quietly and listen, the trees may talk to us without words and convey something of their story."

The two men sat down accordingly and rested a while in silence. Eventually Blake spoke: "I'm sure these trees could tell many a strange tale. Ashton, you are the story-teller. Be their interpreter. What are they saying to you?"

Ashton had been sitting with a meditative, abstracted look as if he were indeed listening to something the other man could not hear. Then in a quiet voice he began to speak:

"I see a man running - a desperate man, a fugitive. Behind him, he knows, is a mob that seeks his life. The time is the eighteenth century, when the crime he is accused of has ceased to be a capital offence in law but is still sometimes punished by death in rural areas.

Magistrates may turn a blind eye to such happenings and clergy refuse sanctuary to the victims, as they did to poor Nan Tuck at Buxted Church, saying 'Thou shalt not suffer a witch to live.'

Yes, the man is accused of witchcraft. The old religion is still practiced in Sussex. Its invocations are chanted on moonlit nights within the fairy rings upon the turf of the Downs. In thatched cottages, a secret cupboard holds forbidden things - a crystal ball, a curiously carved wand, an old black-hilted knife;

perhaps even some time-darkened images of the gods of an elder faith. On certain occasions, these things are brought out - on the nights of the Great Sabbats of Halloween, Candlemas, Beltane and Lammas.

This man has danced at those Sabbats. Indeed, he has presided over the ritual, sometimes out on the hills on a starry summer night, sometimes in winter when the cottage floor is cleared, the fire built up and the curtains well drawn.

But someone has been indiscreet; or perhaps a new vicar has come to the district, a stern fanatic full of hellfire preaching, who has played on the fears and superstition of the ignorant until he has raised a dangerous mob. Somehow, the whisper of suspicion has grown into a storm. The man knows he must not be caught. As the leader, he knows the real names of all the coven not just the nicknames by which they are called at the Sabbat. His heart would never betray them; but flesh and blood may be weakened by torment into speech, or they might betray themselves by some hopeless attempt to rescue him. He must flee fast and far; and some instinct takes him to the sanctuary of the old gods.

Almost exhausted, he has outdistanced his pursuers; but he knows they are still following. He leans his back against one of the biggest tree-trunks and closes his eyes. The scent of earth and leaves comes to him mingled with that of his own sweat. Here in the pagan wild are the forces of life, dark, mysterious, like the roots of the yew-tree sinking deep down into the earth, the body of the primordial mother of all. Here he fears not to die, for all things are born and die and are reborn again, as the earth goes through her seasons, so why not man?

He wants no part of the church people's religion. Their church is built upon a pagan sacred mound. An old standing stone from that mound is built into its foundations, did this new-fangled preacher but know it. And the old Green Man, the spirit of the woods, grins from carven bench-end and roof-boss - aye, right above the preacher's head! The man has looked up at

that carving many a time; but now he doubts if he will ever see
it again.

The spirit of the woods! The god that breathes out the new
life of spring, when the sap rises in the green buds. The weary
man somehow feels kinships with that power; wordless,
nameless, yet with a thousand names of bygone time. He feels
the bole of the trees at his back, alive, a living thing that has
endured for centuries. He invokes, not in words but from his
very soul, the ancient gods in the twilight of that place, upon
the threshold of death.

And even as a hue and cry sounds in the distance, with a
trampling of pursuing feet and horses' hooves, within his soul
there rises up an answer. For there are realms of the twilight
borderland and gates of the elemental powers; and these too
have their rulers and their guardians. There are inner kingdoms
of nature, as well as those that mortal eyes can see; and this
man is called and summoned to pass within and the gate is
opened for him.

He turns slowly around to face the tree and holds up his arms
as if parting a curtain or veil. There is a shimmering of light and
a wild music of unearthly sound. The living body of the tree
and the living body of the man dissolve magically and mingle
together, even as in antique Hellas the limbs of Daphne became
laurel-boughs as she fled from Apollo, or as the nymphs called
Dryads could be now a woman and now vanish into an oak.

Furiously the pursuers approach, led by the preacher mounted
on his horse; but the mystery of metamorphosis is done. The
gate between the worlds has closed. Yet still some power lingers
there; for as the preacher gains the path that leads into the trees
of the outer grove, his horse shies at something invisible and
bolts, refusing to enter that haunted shade. Instead, the animal
careers wildly across the heath and out of sight, its rider
shouting and tugging at the reins. The mob straggle after them,
until they find the horse panting and wild-eyed beneath a tree
and the preacher stark dead upon the ground with a broken

neck. A branch, it seems, has struck him from the saddle. The witch-hunt is ended."

Ashton had been speaking almost like a man in a trance. Now he ceased and fell silent, looking down at the black earth at their feet. Blake looked at him questioningly. Had he indeed become attuned to some events of the past?

"That was quite a story," Blake remarked. Ashton lifted his head sharply as if to shake off some influence. "Yes, indeed," he replied. "You see what fantasies can be inspired by reverie in a place like this? But come, we'll walk on and I'll show you the rest of the grove. Some of the biggest trees are still ahead."

They went forwards along the path, which was sometimes overgrown now, so that they had to pick their way between writhing branches. Emerging into a wider pathway beneath huge and venerable trees, Blake marvelled anew at the strange symmetry and power of their shapes. Looking at them, one could see the primitive life-force of the earth rising and solidifying into form. In spite of their age, here and there around the bases of the trunks young shoots had sprung forth, full of rich dark green leaves. Blake ran his hands through the foliage. He too was beginning to attune to this place.

Suddenly he stopped and pointed to where a shaft of sunlight fell upon one of the trees.

"Good God, Ashton, look there!"

Ashton started round at Blake's exclamation. "What is it?"

"Can't you see it? Look there, where I'm pointing!"

"I see nothing," Ashton said, surprised at his friend's agitation. Blake pointed his walking-stick towards the patch of light and shadow.

"Come and stand here. You'll see it plainly. Every detail is there."

Ashton stood beside Blake and looked closely at what his friend was indicating. Now indeed he too could see plainly the strange sight that had startled Blake. Like a piece of sculpture, but wrought by no human hands, there appeared upon the wood of that mighty and ancient tree a form. It was the nude figure of a man, facing towards the tree-trunk as if in the act of disappearing within it. The head had already vanished within. The arms were blending into the wood, held out as if parting a curtain. The shape of the back muscles, the proportion of the thighs and legs, were all correctly delineated. Yet what they saw could be nothing but the natural growth of the tree. Ashton stared at it and seemed even more amazed than Blake.

"I have never seen that before," he said in a low voice. "And yet it is the figure of my story."

"You mean you never heard that story before? Nor ever read of it?" Blake queried.

"Never," Ashton replied. "It came to me as the sheerest fantasy, unfolding itself before my mind's eye. And now we find this."

"Where is the head of the figure?" asked Blake. "It seems to be sunk into the tree. But there is a head. Look there, above!"

They looked upwards, to a gnarled branch gilded by a thin ray of the afternoon sun. In the shape of the wood, a face looked down at them; but it was not a human face. It was broad, satyr-like, with huge deep eyes, flat nose and grinning mouth.

"The Green Man," said Ashton. "The old god of the woods. Here he was invoked; and here his mark remains."

They looked long and silently upon the forms within the living wood. Then they continued in thoughtful mood their walk through that ancient grove, until they emerged again into the sunlight, the open heathland and the song of birds.

Doreen Valiente

# A Night In Wookey Hole

"It is not often," said Ashton, "that one finds anything of real interest in a secret drawer. But I did find something once – a manuscript. You may care to see it."

The two friends, Ashton and Blake, were spending a weekend together at Ashton's Sussex cottage. Young Blake was somewhat depressed. A love-affair which had seemed to promise him great things had ended disastrously, with the lady's elopement with another man. He sat glumly by Ashton's log fire, while Ashton, who knew most of what had happened, kindly refrained from asking him for any details, but instead sought about for something to entertain him and take his mind off his troubles.

Accordingly, Ashton had been telling Blake about the fine furniture and objects of art he had encountered in the course of his life as an antique dealer. Some of the most interesting pieces he had kept for himself when he retired, in order to furnish his country home. These now reflected the firelight in Ashton's cosy living room as he invited Blake to picture the scenes they had once been part of. That little chair, for instance, adapted to the spreading skirts of a crinoline – what lovely lady had once occupied it? The row of gleaming pewter plates, which shone softly against the dark oak panelling – what company so long ago had gathered to eat from them? And as for that fine old desk, two centuries old at least, see how many beautifully made drawers it has – including the secret drawer!

Thus Ashton had brought the conversation around to the subject of finds in secret hiding-places and eventually succeeded in arousing Blake's interest.

"Is that the desk you found this thing in?" Blake asked.

"No," said Ashton. "But it was a very similar one; a fine piece which came from an old vicarage. I don't think that the people who sold it to me knew it had a secret drawer. I thought it might have, though, because of its resemblance to this one; so when I got it home from the saleroom I examined it closely and found I was right. Inside the drawer was a tightly folded package of papers, yellowed with age and covered with faded writing. It bore no date, unfortunately; but from the texture of the paper and the style of the writing I judged it to be of the eighteenth century and the internal evidence of the story it contains supports this view. I would say the events described took place in the earlier part of that century and were evidently written down some years afterwards."

"May I see it?" Blake requested.

"Certainly," said Ashton. "But it's quite a long tale and closely written. I suggest we have dinner first."

Ashton, who was an excellent cook, busied himself with preparing and serving a simple but first-class meal. The Sussex chicken, which had been gently roasting in the oven, was set out on the antique dining table, which had its highly polished surface well protected with decorative mats for the occasion. Locally grown fresh vegetables accompanied the meal, which was served upon plates and dishes that had once graced an old manor house. The table was lit with candles in Georgian silver candlesticks, which revealed the shine and sparkle of Ashton's best white wine in long-stemmed crystal goblets.

Under such genial influences, Blake's gloomy mood was rapidly lifting. By the end of the dessert, which was apple pie and cream, he was positively cheerful. Ashton, however, firmly refused his offer to help wash up, telling him to go and relax by the fire instead. Privately, Ashton preferred to handle the fine china and glass himself and see it safely put away, before entering upon after-dinner conversation.

"Now," said Blake when all was safely cleared away and they had reached the fireside coffee stage, "what about this mysterious manuscript?"

From a drawer of the antique desk, Ashton produced a wad of folded papers and handed them to Blake. The latter examined the papers under the light; but soon said, "I'm afraid this is too much for me. The writing's so faded and there are all these old-fashioned long S's. I can make out the title; it says *The Narrative of Charles Somerville*; but I think, Ashton you'd better read me the rest, if you will."

"Very well," said Ashton. "I'll just bring the lamp nearer - there, that's better. Now, I told you that the piece of furniture I found this in came from an old vicarage; and the writer, Charles Somerville, seems to have been an Anglican clergyman of the eighteenth century. It's a very queer tale he tells and rather a frightening one. At any rate, it frightened him to such an extent that it changed his whole life, which is why he sets it down. I will take leave to omit a rather long and sermon-like preamble and come to the narrative itself."

Ashton then read aloud as follows, while the logs glowed softly upon the hearth and the wind soughed round the old cottage in the gathering dusk:

"Before I was ordained, nay indeed, before I had any thoughts of entering the Church, I was one of a profligate crew of idle and wealthy young men who gathered around Sir Edward ----- (I suppress the surname, for 'tis that of a notable and ancient family). He was a brilliant and handsome fellow, no worse a drunkard or a libertine than were we all; but there was in him somewhat of a darker nature, in that his pleasure had ever with it an element of cruelty. It had long been evident to me that he found relish in inflicting pain and seeing it inflicted, whether upon man, woman or animal. Partial as I was to elegance of manner, I could scarcely bear to watch him at a public hanging, not jeering and laughing with the mob as the poor wretch danced on air, but smiling as if at some refined entertainment. And yet so engaging were his manners that shortly afterwards

I would take wine with him and laugh myself at the freedom of his wit.

There was another peculiarity of Sir Edward's, which I now recall with anguish; nay, worse than the one I have noted above. It was his humour to mock at the sacred mysteries of religion; and that with such brutal excess that he was a leading figure in those vile societies known as Hellfire Clubs. There was, as we know, a craze for such things at one time, so much so that His Majesty King George I by an Order in Council took action to put an end to the scandal; after which such circles did not, indeed cease their abominations but became somewhat more discreet (nor are they yet extinct at the present day).

It was for his involvement in such dark matters that Sir Edward earned the nickname by which all the town knew him, namely 'Hellfire Ned.' And I, alas, must confess that I and my companions took part in many a bawdy revel over which Hellfire Ned presided, that lasted until the grey dawn rose and shamed the guttering candles. I have been no stranger to bagnios and dens of every vice, under Ned's tutelage. My only aim was pleasure; but with Ned it was something more. I remember well, even bemused as I was with the fumes of wine, how Ned's eyes glittered as he raised his glass in a blasphemous toast to 'the powers of Hell,' while the half-naked wenches who shared our revels laughed and shrieked and some of us grew uneasy at his earnestness

I might have continued indefinitely in this kind of debauchery and come to Heaven knows what ill end, had not that event occurred which I am resolved to set down here. Our roistering crew had grown weary of their usual haunts and were seeking for some new sensation, when we heard from a gentleman who owned an estate in the county of Somerset a description of a most deep and fearful cavern situated in those parts, called Okey Hole. 'Tis mentioned in old Camden's Brittania, wherein he records that the people of that countryside tell many strange stories of the cave.

Our Somerset squire favoured us with a description of the wild ravine in which the cavern is situated, the underground river which rushes forth from the hillside there and the narrow entrance to the cave itself, which entrance is know as Hell's ladder.

This, as you may guess, appealed at once to the fancy of Sir Edward; especially when he heard that it was a custom of the younger and more sportive of the local gentry to carry lanterns, wine and provisions into the cave and make merry there, even bringing with them a fiddler so that the company might have music to dance to.

Sir Edward at once proposed that our next midnight orgy should be held in Okey Hole, or Wookey Hole as the local rustics termed it. And to speak truth, this served our turn very well, for there were several of us who were glad of an excuse to leave town for a while, either to escape debts or because of some falling-out with the law. Sir Edward therefore proposed that we should take coaches to Bath upon pretence of taking the waters and from thence proceed to Wookey Hole in the lonely hills of Mendip. We were promised hospitality by the gentleman who had acquainted us with the existence of the cave, who undertook moreover to guide us to it.

Thus, the weather being good for the journey, before very long we were all assembled in the Squire's hall and ready to proceed with our plans. We had gathered with us as many fair Cyprians or ladies of the town as we could persuade to accompany us. I remember how their gaudy dresses made strange contrast with our own attire; for it was the whim of Hellfire Ned that the men of the company should affect a distinctive costume in mockery of monkish robes, which costume should consist of a long black gown and a hood; and thus were we all clothed. Some of us in addition, ashamed to show their faces in such company, had donned black velvet masks, as also had some of the ladies (or those who hoped to be taken for such).

A gang of servants as disreputable as their masters stood ready to carry the wine and provisions to the cave, from which they would then be bidden discreetly to retire. A villainous-looking fiddler who played at inns and fairs thereabouts had been hired to strike up some bawdy tunes. All was ready but for one circumstance, which caused some remark. Ned was not there.

The leader of our revels had indeed arrived at the Squire's house, but had then excused himself the night before, saying that he had some private business of his own to transact in the neighbourhood and would join us later, in good time for the feast. However, the hour grew late and darkness was gathering, but still no sigh of him. We were constrained to move off without him, in order to gain the entrance to Wookey Hole before nightfall.

How fearful was that ravine, shaded by great trees and with the sound of the rushing waters of the river Axe mingling with the wind in the leaves! There is a paper mill there furnishing employment for a number of artisans; but by now all were gone home from their work and the place was deserted. The Squire's well-distributed coin had discouraged curiosity among the yokels and secured our entrance to the cavern without question. So picking our way by the light of lanterns, we came to that opening in the hillside which gives access to the cave.

The women affected to shriek and hang back, but were pressed by their gallants to enter, the Squire leading the way and telling the company when to bow their heads (for in some places the roof was so low that we could not stand upright). And so we made our way within and downwards in the chill dark.

For my own part, I confess that as soon as I crossed the entrance to that place, terror seized upon my soul; and I believe the others were likewise affected. But being most of us half-tipsy already, we dissembled our fears with loud laughter and jests, mingled with curses as we stumbled on. Our voices echoed through the cavern with a hollow and dismal sound (for "tis of such a vastness within that no man knoweth the full extent of it"). The flickering lights of our lanterns wavered hither and thither, casting fantastic shadows upon the walls and now and then illuminating some peculiar formation of the stalactites and stalagmites which hung from the roof or arose from the floor, formed by the age-long dropping of mineral-impregnated water.

At length we found ourselves at the end of the long downward entrance called Hell's Ladder and in a greater cave, with high roof and beside the stream of that under-ground river which indeed resembles the fabled Styx.

Here the Squire told us to halt. 'For,' said he, 'you are now in the Witch's Kitchen. And behold! Here is the Witch!' Speaking thus, he suddenly directed the rays of his lantern upon a huge, dark mass that loomed before us.

Though I had felt fear before, ever since my entry into these depths, it was less than the sudden and panic fright which seized upon me now. I cried out aloud; and some commotion was caused among us by one of the women fainting. I think several of us would have gone no further, but for the thought of retracing our steps without a guide back up to the cave entrance and out through that benighted ravine. So we calmed our wits as best we might and examined more closely that looming black shape revealed by the lantern's glow.

I realised that it was a gigantic stalagmite, formed upon the floor of the cave by the action of dripping water throughout what must have been thousands of years. In shape, it roughly resembled a statue of that dark goddess whom the ancient Romans called Cybele or the Magna Mater and worshipped with orgiastic rites; a heavy-breasted, brooding figure with the face of an old woman, the head surmounted by a kind of cap. Unlike its surrounding formations, the great stalagmite was black; coloured by the soot of ancient sacrificial fires, so our guide informed us. Seeing the baleful aspect of the thing, I doubted him not. We were, in my opinion, in a sanctuary of our remote ancestors, who untold generations ago had worshipped the great stalagmite as a goddess, formed as it was by natural forces which to them were mysterious and therefore magical. In later years, after Christianity had vouchsafed its light to our islands, the memory of the ancient goddess and the awe which it inspired had shaped itself into legends of the Witch of Wookey, turned to stone when a monk from the nearby Abbey of Glastonbury had sprinkled holy water upon her (a legend still current among the peasantry hereabouts).

There was an air about this sombre form which was far removed from such foolish tales, especially to one who like myself had studied the works of classical authors and allowed his thoughts to wander through the vastness of antiquity which they described. I found myself thinking of the deities of benighted Egypt; of primeval cults underlying the civilisation of the Roman Empire and celebrated with mysterious and darksome rituals; and of the Greek Hecate, goddess of witches, who was invoked at night by the flame of torches and hailed as queen of the phantom-world. My mind reeled and I almost forgot the present time and place, starting when someone laid a hand on my arm to bid me to move on.

'Damn it, we are all struck sober!' yelled a voice from one of my boon companions. 'Let us get on towards the further cave, where we can drink and be merry!' Suiting action to words, he drew me onwards as the whole party continued as hastily as they might into an even vaster cavern, where we were to hold our revel. Our ample supply of wine and food was arranged by the servants upon a great stone which served as a table. Our lanterns were disposed around the cave, giving a flickering and uncertain light in contract to the unknown darkness beyond. Then the lackeys withdrew and the fiddler struck up a merry tune. The fainting lady and her fair companions were revived with strong drink till they declared themselves quite recovered and proved it by joining in the dance. Soon all was mirth and licentious revelry, from which only our leader, Hellfire Ned, was missing.

A mock throne, resembling a Master Mason's chair, had been erected in the cave for Ned to occupy; for such was the common form of our rowdy assemblies. One of the oldest and most hardened sinners amongst us pointed to it and said he doubted not that Ned would soon be with us. 'For,' said he with an evil leer, 'I know what his *private business* is. He is out hunting a pretty little doe; and he has promised us such an account of the chase as shall divert us all.'

This was greeted with a general roar of laughter and approval; for in sooth our spirits had been somewhat lowered by Sir Edward's absence. Our bold wenches, heated by drink and dancing, threw off their garments and cavorted naked but for shoes and stocking; a state which the lusty revellers were not slow to take advantage of. Nay, shame restricts my pen from describing all the scenes of that night – scenes which came soon enough to a hideous climax.

I have written already how Ned was wont to drink a toast to 'the Powers of Hell.' Weary of waiting, one reckless blade made bold to imitate him. Raising his glass on high, he invited us to drink Ned's health and Ned's toast: 'To the Powers of Hell!'

Even as his voice rang around the dark places of the cavern, a strange and hollow echo seemed to follow it, a melancholy and fearful sound as if welling up for the black gulfs beyond our circle of light. Then it grew into a terrible ululation, roaring through the whole labyrinth of the caves like the voices of those dreaded phantoms that rage through the air across desolate places and are called the Wild Hunt. I cannot convey the terror of those sounds. It was as if hell itself had suddenly opened its loathsome gates and permitted the triumphant voices of fiends to be borne to us upon a ravening wind. I flung myself upon the ground and put my hands over my ears; but I could still hear the screams and curses of those around me, mingled with the vibrating roar from the unknown.

The Squire who had brought us thither yelled above the tumult, trying frantically to restrain the general panic.

'Hold, hold!' he cried. ''Tis naught but the voice of the caverns. I tell you these sounds are often heard. Calm yourselves, I say!'

When some measure of order was restored. He assured us that such fearful and mysterious noises had been heard in the caves from time immemorial. Twas believed that they proceeded from some motion of the waters of the underground river in the labyrinthine depths beyond. True, on this occasion they had been uncommonly fearsome; but their cause was surely a natural one. Men of sense and spirit should not be affrighted by them.

At this, we made shift to recover and laugh at our fears, as the dreadful sounds died away; though some of the women were still whimpering and many a man's hand shook as he poured himself another glass. Then someone cried, 'Ha, here is the crown of our feast! Here is that which shall renew our mirth! Look, Ned is among us at last!' And he pointed to the throne-like chair from which Hellfire Ned was wont to preside over us, which had hitherto stood empty.

Looking in that direction, I saw in the dim light (for some of the lanterns had been overset in the previous confusion) that this place was indeed now occupied. A figure was seated in it, clad in a long black monkish robe as were the rest of us, but with the hood drawn up over the head so that the face was invisible. I was fairly near to the throne, near enough for what I saw to give me some unease. The black-clad form sat upright, stiff and still; and I fancied that a coldness seemed to emanate from it. Was it indeed Sir Edward – or another? For a moment, an awful speculation presented itself to my mind, that it was an evil spirit come in answer to that blasphemous invocation and that those hideous sounds had been the heralds of its coming.

With the figure's continued silence and stillness, a similar unease to my own seemed to spread itself throughout the assembled company. At length, someone called out nervously, 'How do you, Ned?' There was no answer. Again, in a voice high-pitched with fright, the caller repeated his question. 'Ned! How – how do you, Ned?'

Then very slowly the figure rose to its feet and pulled back the hood of its sombre robes. There was revealed to us the face of Sir Edward, dabbled with blood and with the look of death upon it. It was the face of a corpse which yet walked the earth. And even as I stared horror-stricken at it, that ghastly and livid countenance contorted itself into an expression of the most terrible despair, while there seemed to come these answering words in Ned's voice, not from the grimacing lips but out of the air as if borne upon some spectral wind:

*'I am dead! Dead and damned!'*

The echoes of this mournful utterance murmured around the cavern, till they seemed to waken again and mingle with those other sounds that had so affrighted us before. Again there arose those awesome clamours from the unknown; and this time their dread reverberations were such that we could bear no more. Our nerve was fairly broken and a general exodus ensued. The hardier spirits seized lanterns and scattered garments and somehow managed to scramble back to the entrance, dragging with them the rest, amid indescribable confusion, yells and screams, as we fought to get out of that accursed place.

How I myself attained the exit I do not know. I have no clear recollection of it; the last impression vivid upon my mind, as it will be to my dying day, was of what I saw just before that desperate flight. I have related how I was near enough to the black-robed apparition of Sir Edward to see it clearly – would that I had not! For as my gaze was fixed upon it and those fearful words were uttered, a change yet more evil came upon that countenance that was already evil enough. Its features seemed to melt and collapse like a waxen puppet tortured over a witch's fire. They ran together and fell in upon each other in an unspeakable transformation. The whole body seemed to fall in upon itself as if a semi-liquescent decay had suddenly seized upon it. It shrank and disintegrated until there was nought left but an appearance as of black smoke that mingled with the shadows and was gone.

When our bedraggled company at last foregathered at the Squire's house, the grey dawn was breaking, revealing us to each other pallid and dishevelled like so many ghosts ourselves. We found that fearful news awaited us. Sir Edward was indeed dead. His confidential manservant had arrived to impart the facts to us privately, which he did to the Squire and a few gentlemen, of whom I was one, behind locked doors in the Squire's library.

It transpired that Sir Edward had made a lewd wager with some of his most intimate friends, that upon his visit to Somerset he would have his will of a certain lady of quality who was the wife of a high-ranking Army officer. He had met the lady in London society and made advances to her which had been firmly repulsed, for she was virtuous as well as beautiful. This circumstance had piqued Sir Edward's pride, for it was ever his boast that he could have any woman he lusted after. Accordingly he had set his lackeys to spy upon the lady's movements and had thus discovered that her husband had a country house in Somerset, where she sometimes resided, not far from the city of Wells. Thereafter he had made his wagerthat the lady should yield to him whether she would or no. 'For,' says he, 'I know when her plaguey husband will be away upon his military duties. I have bribed the rascal butler to make the rest of the servants drunk and to leave a door unlocked for me. And I promise you, gentlemen, such an account of the fair victim's screams and struggles as shall amuse you vastly and reconcile you to paying your bets.'

The lecherous villains, for such they were (though all *gentlemen* in their own estimation), had appointed one of themselves to be stakeholder and had drunk to the success of the ravishing, vowing that if its victim were foolish enough to make complaint afterwards they would all swear that Ned had been with them all the time.

The butler, however, had proved to be an even greater rascal than Ned thought him; for having pocketed Ned's gold he proceeded to disclose the whole plot to his master. The latter made hasty contrivance to exchange duties with another; so that when Ned and his lackey gained entrance to the house, they found themselves confronted by the lady's husband, accompanied by two brother-officers and an Army surgeon. Laid ready upon a side table were a brace of well-matched swords and another of duelling pistols. The husband sternly pointed to these and required Sir Edward forthwith to make his choice of weapons and to afford him the satisfaction of a gentleman, adding that the two other officers had come prepared to act as seconds.

Sir Edward, rapidly recovering his composure, with a scornful smile made choice of the swords; for he was a notable swordsman who was reputed to have been the death of several men in such affairs of honour. This time, however, he had met his match. The duel took place there and then in the entrance hall of the house, which was commodious enough for the purpose. Sir Edward ran the Army man through the shoulder, causing much effusion of blood but little permanent damage;

but the other, in spite of his wound, lunged forward and drove his blade into Sir Edward's heart, killing him instantly.

Hearing this story from the manservant's lips, I realise that there could be no doubt of one thing. Namely, that when I had seen that fearful apparition in the cave, Sir Edward's bloodstained corpse had been lying in the wine cellar of that distant house in which it had been hastily concealed. This consideration caused me to think more deeply than I had done hitherto of the mysteries of life and death, shaken as my careless and worldly philosophy already was by the terrible events of that night.

The rank and wealth of all concerned served to hush up the matter. It was given out that Sir Edward had died of a fever; and he was duly interred in the family vault, with a handsome marble monument erected bearing an epitaph which extolled his virtues. For my own part, the memories of that night precluded me from further enjoyment of such company. I changed my life completely to one of sobriety and repentance, coming eventually to be received into the bosom of that Church in which I hope to end my days. Being now of mature years, I have felt it my duty to set down this private history, though with discretion as to whom to reveal the same, in order to confute unbelief and to rebuke the irreligion and wickedness of the times wherein we live; which may Heaven pardon and amend.

Witness mine hand:

CHARLES SOMERVILLE."

Ashton's pleasantly cultured voice ceased and for a while no sounds were heard in the room except the sigh of the wind around the eaves and the ticking of the old clock. Then Blake spoke.

"Do you believe this story, Ashton?"

Ashton laid down the manuscript and rose to replenish the fire, which had burnt low. He resumed his seat in the armchair and answered Blake's question with careful consideration.

"Yes, I do, for a number of reasons. Firstly, Sir Edward had just died a violent death when the apparition was seen. And if anything can be established upon human testimony, it is the fact of ghosts being seen in such circumstances."

"But not, surely, of such a hideous kind?" Blake objected.

"I think," Ashton replied, "that what occurred in this case was a materialization. Yes, I believe such things can be, given the right conditions. Remember where they were and what had been happening. Wookey Hole is undoubtedly, as Somerville realised, a cave sanctuary of ancient worship – just how ancient, we do not know. Such places are full of latent power. And that excited, dancing, fornicating crowd were deliberately engaged in a mockery of the ancient *Orgia* – the word that 'orgies' comes from, you know. Originally, such wild celebrations were part of the rites of ancient religion. I see you smile, Blake; but sometime you must read a rare and remarkable old book I have, *Two Essays on the Worship of Priapus*, by Richard Payne Knight and Thomas Wright. It was privately printed in 1865 – had to be, in those prudish days. But you are broadminded enough to understand it and it will give you an insight into many curious things, including the real origin of the witches' Sabbat. The relevance in this connection is that such *Orgia* raised power. Power which in this case enabled an anguished and newly discarnate entity to manifest. But the materialization could not be maintained. The temporary form melted away and the soul went to its own place – a dark place, I fear."

"I should like to see the cave of Wookey Hole," said Blake. "I seem to have heard of it as a tourist attraction in the West Country."

"Oh, yes," Ashton answered with a smile. "You can see Wookey Hole today with all the comforts a tourist could ask for – electric lighting, car park, cafeteria, guided parties – but think, Blake, of what it must have been like when Somerville saw it! It is wonderful and awesome enough today. I remember going there, surrounded by cheerful holidaymakers; and when I saw the great stalagmite called the Witch of Wookey, in my mind the years rolled back, the things of today faded and I knew myself to be in the presence of the primordial, even as Somerville did. I recalled an old line of Bardic poetry about the Druidic goddess Cerridwen: *The old giantess, darkly smiling in her wrath.* She presided over initiation into the British Mysteries – perhaps in these very caves. You know, Blake, this fire is too good to leave yet. Shall we make a pot of tea?"

Blake gladly assented. The tea was made and the two men talked far into the night, of ancient things and of matters beyond the veil of the unseen, until Blake's previous trouble seemed to him a thing far off and of little account, no longer worth grieving after.

# The Corn Dolly

"Ashton, do you believe in witchcraft? I mean, *really* believe in it?"

Ashton looked up in some surprise as Blake asked the question. The two men had just returned to Ashton's cottage after a visit to a small and very ancient Sussex church, where Ashton had been helping some of his friends and neighbours with the harvest festival decorations. Not that Ashton was a regular churchgoer; but it was typical of him to count among his friends a local vicar, a Rabbi and a Buddhist monk, while retaining his own philosophy of life which he forced upon no one. So he and Blake had spent a pleasantly busy Saturday afternoon under the vicar's enthusiastic direction, holding ladders to arrange garlands, polishing red and green apples, filling vases with water for huge bunches of chrysanthemums and Michaelmas daisies, while the vicar's wife and other lady parishioners dashed around with dusters and shone brasswork. Eventually the fabric of the little old church, much of which dated back to Saxon times, was bright with the simple decorations of the season, as it had been each year for centuries past. The helpers had been refreshed with buttered scones and mugs of tea in the vicarage kitchen and had then gone their several ways home in the gathering dusk and first chill of autumn.

Now Blake and Ashton were settled by a newly-lit fire having a rest and a glass of dry sherry before dinner.

The only topic of conversation in Ashton's mind had been the history of the old church they had just left. Hence his surprise at Blake's question.

"Whatever makes you ask that?" Ashton queried.

"Well," was Blake's response, "it was something I saw in the church - among the decorations, you know. It was a corn dolly."

Ashton eyed Blake keenly. "And that made you think of witchcraft? Well, paganism, perhaps - the old religion of the countryside. The corn dolly woven from the last sheaf of wheat to be harvested, as it used to be in the old days. But our vicar is broad-minded. And you know, making corn dollies has become a regular country craft now. People like to buy them to hang on their walls as an ornament. You see many of the old designs perpetuated in that way; and you know, in the olden days every district had its distinctive design. Let me see, there's the Staffordshire Knot, the Suffolk Horseshoe, the Cambridgeshire Bell, the Herefordshire Fan - Oh, lots of them still survive and the present day's added some new ones. But that one they had in the church was just a simple traditional dolly, woven round a core of straw and finished off with a bunch of ears of wheat and a loop to hang it up by. I thought it looked very well among all the other things. Didn't you like it?"

Blake remained pensive.

"The fact is," he said, "that it reminded me of something. Something very odd that happened a while back. I've never been able to make up my mind about it, whether it was just coincidence or something more sinister."

He watched the flickering firelight thoughtfully for a few moments. Then Ashton broke in.

"Well, Blake, I'm usually the one who tells the stories. But how about hearing this one from you for a change?"

"All right," Blake replied. "Actually, I'd like to have your opinion on it. It concerned a chap who used to work for me. Lewis, his name was. His chief job was driving a van, fetching and delivering. As you can imagine, this took him about the countryside and gave him plenty of opportunities for his favourite pursuit. He was a real Casanova, the sort that couldn't see a woman without making a pass at her, whether she was married or single. He was completely heartless about it. To him it was just a game and he used to regale the other chaps with stories of how he got on. I'm not narrow-minded, I hope, but he used to sicken me. I wished sometimes that the girls he scored with (that was one of his favourite expressions, by the way) could hear how he talked about them afterwards. But he was very good-looking and they seemed to fall for him and believe everything he said. The office was always taking 'phone calls from girls - and sometimes from irate husbands too - wanting to know where he was. He just laughed everything off. And then one day, to my surprise, I heard he was getting married.

She was a really lovely young girl, too. Linda was her name. She was a real village beauty. He showed her photograph proudly around to his mates, saying "I'm marrying this one." I saw the picture, taken when she won some local beauty contest and was crowned Carnival Queen or some such thing. Believe me, if only she had had some brains to match her looks, she could have made a career for herself as a model; even a film star, perhaps. But unfortunately for her, she was a silly, weakly feminine, romantically sentimental type, who could only think of having a beautiful white wedding and living happily ever after - and didn't have the sense to see what sort of a man she was marrying.

Her old mother had summed Lewis up the first time she met him. But Linda was so blindly in love that she could see it was useless to oppose her, so the wedding went ahead. Everyone said what a good-looking couple they made and we held the usual collection for a wedding present from the firm. Then Lewis moved in with Linda and her mother to the lovely old cottage in the village street which Linda's mother owned - and which Lewis had made no secret to his men friends of looking forward to inheriting 'when the old girl kicks the bucket,' as he put it.

Well, the marriage lasted about six months. Then, with Linda pregnant, Lewis's roving eye started to wander and he was soon up to his old tricks again, playing around with other women. Linda's mother caught him at it and there was a row; but Linda wouldn't believe a word against him, or at any rate she wouldn't listen to any. Eventually, though, Linda herself caught him with another girl in circumstances where she couldn't deny the evidence of her own eyes as she opened her own bedroom door. This time there was a really big row. He made it worse by trying to laugh it off, saying the girl was just a little slut who'd hitched a lift with him and it didn't mean a thing. But Linda sobbed until she went into premature labour and lost the baby.

Linda came out of hospital very depressed. Her looks had suffered and her illusions were shattered. She was a changed girl. I'd heard at the office how she had been rushed to hospital, so when I was in their village on business and saw Linda's mother in the main street I stopped the car and asked how Linda was. The old lady invited me home for a cup of tea and poured out the whole story as we sat in the kitchen. Linda was resting in bed upstairs and Lewis was at work so she could speak freely. I think it made her feel better to talk about it and let out some of the fury she had been bottling up inside.

She had good reason to be angry, too. Apparently, she'd had a scene with Lewis while Linda was in hospital and told him what she thought of him. He'd quite calmly replied that he had no intention of changing his ways and that anyway it was all Linda's fault 'for being such a bloody fool as to get pregnant and lose her looks.' The old lady's jaw had set resolutely and her eyes glittered as she told me this. I could see that she wasn't the crying kind and I wondered just what she would do about the situation.

I asked tentatively if Linda was likely to seek a separation from Lewis. They hadn't been married long enough for her to be able to get a divorce yet. The old lady shook her head.

'No,' she said. 'I know Linda is too weak to make up her mind to do that. Oh, she'll cry and say she's through with him and all the rest of it. But when it comes to the point of actually going to a solicitor's office and starting proceedings, she'll hang back. She'll change her mind and say no, maybe, I should give him another chance - and so it will go on. Until she's middle-aged and I'm gone and her life is ruined. Because he won't leave *her*! Oh, no! He wants this house too much and the little bit he knows I've got in the bank. But he'll treat her worse than an animal and then throw her a few false words of love now and again, enough for her to go on pretending she's got a marriage, while she gets more and more broken down and degraded. And she was my lovely daughter!'

The old lady had risen to her feet and was pacing up and down the room as she spoke. Then she stopped and stood gripping the back of an old-fashioned kitchen chair as she stared into the distance.

'No,' she said. 'No, not lawyers and separations. There are other ways. Older ways'.

Then, as if realising that perhaps she had said more than she meant to, she forced a smile and went on, 'But I mustn't burden you too much with our troubles, Mr. Blake. Do have another cup of tea. It was kind of you to call and see us.'

I said I must be going and made the usual small talk about hoping Linda would soon be better and so on. Inwardly I felt desperately sorry for both the girl and her mother; but I wondered as I drove away just what the mother had been on the point of saying about 'older ways.' What could she have meant? I knew that she was a widow and that Linda was her youngest child, born when she herself was middle-aged and loved and spoiled accordingly. There were two much older brothers, both of whom had done well for themselves, one in Australia and one in Canada. Perhaps their mother was thinking of appealing to them to come and help their sister? But I knew it wasn't so easy, when people were a long way away and they had their own homes and businesses to attend to. Besides, I felt pretty sure somehow that this wasn't what Linda's mother had been thinking of at all.

It was not long afterwards that I found out what her words had really meant. And when I did, it was by accident. Lewis was usually just efficient enough at his job to keep out of trouble. We'd established long ago just how much nonsense I would stand for from him and he seldom over-stepped the mark with me. However, on this day we were waiting for some stuff he was supposed to deliver and he was nowhere to be found. I guessed that he was either in a pub somewhere or fooling around with some girl as usual. I sat in my office making 'phone calls in search of him and fuming because they were getting me nowhere, until eventually I decided to try his home.

The cottage had no telephone, so I got out my car and drove over. I had to leave the car in the village car park, as parking was banned in the narrow old street. So I proceeded to the cottage on foot and rang the front door bell, thinking as I did every time I saw the old roof and the whitewashed walls what a dear, quaint little place it was - late seventeenth century at a guess and beautifully kept. However, on this day the bell seemed to be out of order. I couldn't make anyone hear, so I went around the side to knock on the back door. As I did so I passed nthe kitchen widow and glanced inside.

Ashton, for the first time in my life I found myself witnessing a scene of witchcraft! The two women, Linda and her mother, were seated in the kitchen with the door shut. Both had their attention focused upon the object on the kitchen table, so intently that they had not realised I was there. For my part, I was so startled and amazed at the scene before me that I hastily drew back out of sight and continued watching through the edges of the net curtains.

I could see Linda slumped disconsolately in a chair by the open fire. She looked a mere shadow of the smart pretty girl she used to be before her marriage. Only her eyes were alert as they stared at what her mother was doing. The old lady was seated at the table in the middle of the room. Before her was a lighted candle set in a curious candlestick which seemed to be made out of a piece of very old polished bone. The candle, I noticed, was black. There were a few other things on the table. I couldn't see them all; but the main things were this black candle, an old knife or perhaps some sort of ceremonial dagger and right in the centre a corn dolly. Around the things on the table was a length of scarlet cord, draped so as to form a circle.

The dolly was quite a simple one, just an oval-shaped container of woven straw with a few ears of wheat decorating it at one end. It looked newly made, presumably on purpose for this ceremony. The old woman was muttering over it and making signs over it with the knife. Her face showed complete concentration of malevolent will. Then she took up from a little dish a large, old-fashioned black-headed pin, passed it through the candle-flame and stuck it into the dolly, saying some form of words as she did so. More pins followed, each time passed through the flame and accompanied by the repetition of the spell. Her actions were careful, deliberate and in the most deadly earnest. The thickness of the glass prevented me from hearing what she was saying; but it seemed to be a sing-song incantation, a sort of sinister nursery rhyme.

How long this would have gone on, I do not know; but I had counted seven pins before suddenly there was a voice which I could hear clearly. Linda had leaped to her feet, half-shouting, 'Oh, what the hell's the use?'

The old woman swayed back, startled, as Linda grabbed the corn dolly and swung it above her head. Her face was convulsed with fury and frustration. 'Curse him!' she screamed. 'Curse him for what he's done to me! Damn him, damn him, the rotten bastard!' Her pent-up rage poured out in a torrent of incoherent words as she flung the corn dolly violently towards the fireplace.

It caught fire and fell down half-burnt upon the hearth. The old woman said no more, only watched Linda with glowing eyes. The dolly had split open, revealing some sort of stuffing inside it; straw and something else besides. Linda ground it under her heel and then kicked it into the fire, where it blazed up and finally fell to ash. She stood staring at it, her hands clenched, as it burned.

I felt sickened and horrified. Embarrassed too, somehow, not only at witnessing a scene of savage superstition out of the middle ages, but of seeing the raw private emotions of two human beings. I abandoned any idea of enquiring about Lewis and tiptoed away before they knew I was there.

It was about a week later that I was again sitting in my office waiting for Lewis to turn up with the van and wondering where he was. He had eventually appeared with a plausible excuse the time before; but I was getting fed up with this. I was turning over in my mind what to do about it when the phone rang. Ah, Lewis at last, I thought. But it wasn't; it was the police.

They were sorry to have to tell me that there had been a serious accident to one of our vehicles. At least, they thought it was one of ours. They would be glad if I could come over and help them to identify the vehicle and the driver.

It sounded pretty bad - three vehicles involved in a crash on a country road. I got out my car and drove over there as fast as I could. When I got near to the scene of the crash an ambulance passed me, going in the other direction. Ahead, I could see a police road-block, various emergency vehicles with flashing lights and behind them a sinister lingering cloud of black smoke. On the grass verge, a casualty was being attended to. A police officer held up his hand to stop me. I explained who I was and he let me through.

I remember what a lovely sunny afternoon it was. All around, there were peaceful green fields, big leafy trees - and in the middle of it all, horror and sudden death. It had been one of those crazy, head-on smashes that just shouldn't happen and does. Apparently, Lewis had been speeding, probably because he knew he was late. We learned later that he'd been in a pub and probably had just enough drink to make him reckless and to interfere with his concentration. Then he'd found himself hemmed in behind one of those big, slow, clumsy-looking pieces of farm machinery that you see sometimes moving on country roads. He'd been too impatient to wait until he could see properly around it - just took a chance and swung out to overtake. And there had been another farm vehicle, a massive great tractor, coming the other way.

He'd tried desperately to take evasive action; but at the speed he was doing it was too late. The van had hit the tractor, gone spiraling off, crashed and then burst into flames. The chap in the ambulance had been the driver of the tractor. He had cuts, bruises and shock, but nothing too serious. The driver of the farm vehicle was the casualty by the side of the road. He looked white and shaken but apparently otherwise unhurt. He'd managed to get to the nearest house and call for help before collapsing from shock.

Our van was a smoking wreck, with firemen working on it with cutting gear. You could just make out half of one of the number plates and part of our name on the side. The police wouldn't let me get too near it. They just wanted to know if I could definitely identify the vehicle and tell them who had been driving it. There was no point in asking me or anyone else if they could identify Lewis. They did it eventually through his dental records."

Blake sipped his sherry and fell silent. For a few moments neither man had anything to say, mentally reliving that ghastly scene. Then Blake looked up at Ashton and spoke again.

"Look here, Ashton, what I want to know - well, that thing I saw through the kitchen window. The old woman sticking pins into the corn-dolly. *Could* that possibly have had anything to do with Lewis's death? Or is it just insane superstition? Sometimes I've thought one way and sometimes the other. I've never discussed it with anyone before. But I'm asking you now. Was Lewis's death just coincidence? Or did that old woman kill him?"

"No," said Ashton reflectively, "I don't think the old woman killed him. I think Linda did."

"*Linda?*" Blake was genuinely shocked. "What on earth do you mean?"

"Well," Ashton replied, "from your description of what you saw, it sounds as if the old lady was a genuine witch. Probably an hereditary one. Which means, among other things, that Linda, although unconsciously, had the same heritage. Linda's mother made and consecrated the corn dolly. I've heard of these things being used in this way before, just as other witches use wax or clay images. And I'll bet that inside that dolly there was something that had been close to Lewis. Combings from his hair, perhaps; nail cuttings; a piece of his clothes. Something that would make the magical link."

"You know, you're absolutely right!" Blake interrupted. "When the dolly broke open, I saw a scrap of material inside. It looked like a piece from a man's shirt."

"Yes," Ashton continued. "The old lady started the ritual. But it was her daughter that brought it to its deadly climax.

"The magical link had been made. But you know, Blake, there has to be real passion behind a thing like this in order to make it work. The mother had what you might call the technical knowledge. But it was Linda who had been stricken to her soul by what this man did to her. Weak, gentle little Linda - probably never initiated or trained as a witch. She didn't have the heart to divorce him. But in that moment, Blake, when she cursed him and hurled the corn dolly into the flames, when the pain and anger within her blazed up like the fire as she remembered her defiled love and her dead baby - in that moment, she had the heart to kill him. And so she did!"

# The Black Dog

The autumn day was darkening into night as Jeremy Blake drove his car rather wearily down yet another winding Sussex lane, cursing the mischievous village boys or whoever it was that had knocked the arms off the signpost. There was no doubt of it, he was well and truly lost.

His business had entailed a trip to a rather remote building site in an unfamiliar part of the county, where he had stayed much longer than he had originally intended. Now here he was, having to find his way out of this maze of lanes, beautiful though they were with the russet tints of autumn leaves and the hawthorn berries that had gleamed fiery red in the rays of the setting sun. But now it was really dark and the moon was rising over the fields and woods that bordered this long lane. There was nothing for it but to keep on until he came to a main road and could find some directions.

He had reached a point in the lane where a thick wood lay on the left hand side, while on the right were fields bordered with hedgerows which had occasional gateways in them to give passage to farm vehicles. As he drew level with the wood, going slowly and carefully down the narrow, unfamiliar lane, he saw a movement by the roadside on his left. There was something there, something blacker than its dark surroundings.

Then he braked hastily as an animal of some kind loped across the road right in front of him. A calf? A small donkey? No, a huge black dog. Just before it vanished under his front wheels, it had turned its head and its eyes had reflected the light, seeming almost to glow of themselves. The reflection of his headlights, he supposed.

An animal-lover himself, Blake hoped profoundly that he had not hit the dog. He got out of his car and looked around with the aid of an electric torch. There had been no feeling of impact, certainly; nor were there any traces of blood on the car or on the road, to Blake's great relief. But where, then, had the animal disappeared to?

It suddenly occurred to Blake that the whole experience was strange and rather eerie. For one thing, the incident had been completely silent. The only sound had been that of the car's brakes. Would not a real dog have made some outcry? Especially as had it been a real dog Blake could scarcely have missed it.

He stood still in the dark lane. The wind rustled among the trees of the wood, coldly and with a hint of frost in it. The bright silver of the waning moon only seemed to make the shadows blacker. There was no gleam of a lighted window anywhere. He seemed to be the only human being in a wilderness of benighted countryside, where strange things prowled after the sun was set.

A wailing cry from the dark depths of the wood made him start. It was nothing but an owl; but somehow its voice seemed the essence of loneliness. Hastily, he got back into the car. He wanted lights and fellow humans around him, quickly.

Driving as fast as he dared down the lane, he was at length gratified to see a crossroads ahead of him. Better still, on the right just before the crossroads was the cheerful glow of a fair-sized country inn.

Blake had pulled into the forecourt, tired, hungry and hoping for food and drink as well as directions, before he glanced up at the signboard. When he did so, it was with a slight shock at the coincidence. For the sign said: "*The Black Dog*".

However, there was nothing sinister about the appearance of the pub itself. It seemed quite modern, well-lit and indeed promising food. Soon Blake was seated in a cheerful, well-appointed saloon bar with a generous plateful of ham sandwiches and a mug of good draught lager. He warmed himself at the open fire, noted that the horse-brasses and the copper warming-pans which decorated the walls were all modern fakes (for Ashton had by now trained him to be knowledgeable in such matters) and started chatting to the landlord.

He was soon able to sort out his best route home, with the landlord's help and that of the other customers in the bar, who readily proffered friendly advice. All went very pleasantly until in passing Blake mentioned the incident of the dog in the lane. Did anyone round here, he asked, own such a dog, because he had nearly run over him?

There ensued one of those awkward silences in which the last speaker knows that he has made some kind of *faux pas*, though he knows not why. The landlord's wife, who was polishing glasses with a clean cloth, stopped still for a moment and then said, "Oh, no!" She abruptly retreated to the other end of the bar, evidently disinclined for further conversation; while the landlord brusquely denied any knowledge of the dog. The rest of the company, after a pause, began to talk of other subjects - rather too eagerly, Blake thought.

He duly found his way home in safety, remaining somehow puzzled and intrigued by the whole incident. He had a feeling that there was something queer at the back of it. Accordingly, at his next visit to Ashton's cottage he recounted the story and asked Ashton's opinion of it.

Ashton considered the matter, relaxing in his usual fireside armchair. Then he spoke quietly and rather gravely:

"It sounds to me as if you have seen Black Shuck."

"What on earth is that?" queried Blake.

"The phantom black dog," Ashton answered. "The hound of hell, some old tales call him. He has been haunting Britain for a great many years and there are tales of him in most English counties, particularly in East Anglia; but he's known in Sussex, too."

"What, the same black dog?" Blake asked skeptically.

"We do not really know," Ashton replied. "All we can say is that English folklore is full of tales of hauntings by what I would suggest are elemental spirits taking the form of a spectral black hound with fiery eyes, exactly as you have described."

"What was it you called him - Black Shuck?" Blake asked, a little surprised that Ashton should take an old wives' tale so seriously.

"That is correct," said Ashton. "The name comes from an Anglo-Saxon word *scucca*, meaning a demon. The tales about him vary from one county to another. Sometimes he is regarded as a fearful portent of evil, sometimes as the punisher of evil-doers. Another old name for him is Padfoot, from his habit of following travellers on lonely roads. Do you know that rather terrifying verse from Coleridge's Rime of the Ancient Mariner:

> *Like one that on a lonesome road*
> *Doth walk in fear and dread,*
> *And having once turned round walks on,*
> *And turns no more his head;*
> *Because he knows, a frightful fiend*
> *Doth close behind him tread.*

I wonder if Coleridge was inspired by the folklore of Black Shuck?"

"You are trying to frighten me," said Blake uneasily. "I don't believe in demons. At least I never have done. But I must admit I felt queer when that thing turned its eyes on me. And those people in the pub knew something, I'm sure, though they weren't letting on."

"Yes, about that pub," Ashton mused. "You say it was modern; but you know, it could have been built on the site of a much older pub. There are plenty of places like that, especially near a crossroads." Then a sudden thought seemed to strike him; but whatever it was, he kept it to himself.

"Look here," said Blake, "let's have a ghost-hunt! I mean," he continued, as Ashton looked up in surprise, "I'm pretty sure I could find that lane again and you've roused my interest in these things. I was a fool to be scared. Perhaps I've found an authentic haunting."

Inwardly, Blake felt a certain pride in the thought. After all, why should old Ashton have all the interesting experiences? This time, he too had a tale to tell. Yes, he would follow it up, he told himself, emboldened by the warm, familiar surroundings of Ashton's living room with its bright log fire. The chill of the dark had faded and given way to curiosity.

What exactly did you have in mind?" Ashton asked rather dubiously.

"Well, Blake replied, "I thought we could drive down there sometime after dark, park the car and keep watch. Midnight is the witching hour, I believe. On a fine clear night, of course. No point in messing about in the rain. We might even try to photograph the thing."

"I doubt if we should succeed in doing that," said Ashton. "Although some very odd things do sometimes appear on photographs - psychic extras, researchers call them. But they usually happen spontaneously, often when the person who takes the photograph sees nothing unusual. The trouble is that you would have to use a flash-bulb after dark, which would probably disperse the apparition. Unless you could get hold of some infra-red film and I don't know how to set about that."

"Neither do I," Blake admitted. "Still, I'm game for a midnight vigil if you are."

"You know, Blake," said Ashton, "the occult is a serious subject. I mean, we are touching the edge of the unknown here. If you are really keen to investigate, I will certainly come with you. But strictly on the condition that we take it seriously and that you will be prepared to accept some guidance from me if necessary."

"Of course," Blake agreed. "You know I value your judgment on these things."

Plans were discussed accordingly, bearing in mind the darkening nights as the moon waned. In view of this, it was felt that no time should be lost, so the very next night, weather permitting, was agreed on for the rendezvous. They would have a late dinner at Ashton's cottage and then proceed to the lane, intending to be on watch by midnight. At Ashton's earnest request, Blake told no one else about the venture, to forestall the interference of silly pranksters.

The next day dawned with fair weather and Blake felt a suppressed excitement as the sunset darkened into night and the sky slowly filled with frosty stars.

The two men enjoyed their usual excellent meal, though with only a very moderate amount of wine in view of the occasion and the need to drive Blake's car. Then they prepared to set off for their vigil, taking with them a couple of warm rugs, a good electric torch and a hip-flask of brandy as an additional precaution against the cold.

They drove carefully down the dark winding lanes and eventually arrived at the scene of Blake's strange adventure. The pub called the Black Dog had just closed and the last customers had bid each other goodnight, by the time Blake and Ashton parked their car quietly in a lay-by further up the lane and prepared themselves to wait.

It was a dark night with a rising wind and little illumination but the stars. At first they could see nothing; but after a while their eyes grew accustomed to the dark and the shapes of woodland and hedgerow could be discerned. A light shone in the distance from the inn; but presently that too disappeared. Country folk do not keep late hours. Only a few cars passed them, their headlights seeming to leave a deeper dark behind.

The noises of the night creatures came faintly to them in the quiet; a barking fox, the calling of owls from the wood, some indistinct rustlings in the hedgerow. Above, the constellations wheeled in their age-old procession. Even Blake could pick out the seven bright stars of the Plough; but he could only wonder at the glittering splendour of the rest of that starry dome, so seldom seen by the dwellers in lighted towns.

Eventually, however, continued inaction began to bore Blake. Nothing unusual had manifested itself. Should they leave the car, he suggested, and take a walk down the lane?

Ashton agreed and they walked as quietly as they could towards the inn. Somehow, they seemed fearful of breaking the midnight stillness which had descended on the place. They passed the point at which the dog had appeared before, without incident save that the lane seemed dismal and chill. Then coming towards the inn, Blake saw something which he had not noticed before. The inn had another, separate signboard, planted on the grass verge which at this point was slightly wider than elsewhere.

As they came closer to it, Blake realised that the sign was remarkably large and high. He could not understand how he had not seen it before. It was a queer shape, too; nothing like the sign which had told him the inn's name. He pointed it out to his companion.

"Look, Ashton, what a strange sign It looks something like a gallows. You'd almost think there was a man hanging from it, too. My God," he cried in sudden alarm, "it *is* a man hanging!"

Ashton looked where Blake was pointing. Then as Blake moved hastily towards the ghastly sight, Ashton seized his arm.

"Come back, Blake!" he said sharply. But Blake pulled free. "Damn it, Ashton," he cried, "we've got to cut him down! He can't have been there long." He ran closer to the gallows foot; but Ashton swiftly followed and held him back.

"He has been there a long time," Ashton said in a low voice. "A very, very long time. Look again."

The burden of the gallows slowly turned in the night wind. An almost fleshless skull looked down upon them from empty eye-sockets. Tattered rags of clothes covered the remains, with here and there a dry white bone showing through. The body was suspended in a kind of iron cage hanging from chains. And as Blake halted in horror and amazement, there came faintly upon the breeze a sickly-sweet smell of death which Ashton, who had been through the Second World War, knew only too well.

Blake stared as if hypnotized at the grinning skull.

It seemed to him that a greenish spectral luminescence was growing about the thing and gathering in the eye-sockets.

"Come away, Blake!" said Ashton in the same sharp tone he had used before. His voice seemed to shatter the spell under which Blake was falling. "Look again! he repeated urgently. "There's nothing there!"

And indeed, the evil phantasm had vanished; it seemed to Blake as if a kind of sudden shift of his consciousness had taken place, or some alteration of his sense of sight, as Ashton touched him. But he felt so profound a shock to his nerves that, had Ashton not held his arm, he would have sunk to the ground.

With Ashton supporting him, Blake turned back towards the car, when suddenly a hideous howl came from the shadowed wood. It seemed to echo in Blake's brain, as a huge jet-black hound bounded into the road before them and stood barring their way, glaring at them with fiery eyes and savage fangs bared for attack.

The panic-stricken thought came to Blake that the demon hound had deliberately allowed them to pass earlier, in order to trap them. He felt terror welling up like a dark wave to overwhelm him. Then Ashton drew himself up and raised his free arm in a commanding gesture as if to ward off the apparition, crying out in a voice that Blake had never heard him use before:

*"In the name of Elohim Gibor, be there restriction unto the powers of darkness!"*

A blast of cold air roared through the trees. Then the lane was empty. There was nothing on the road before them but the faint gleam of starlight.

How Blake regained the car he scarcely knew. He was dimly aware of Ashton supporting his arm; and when they did arrive back at the place where they had parked, the latter insisted that Blake took a few good mouthfuls from the flask of brandy. "I'm going to drive, anyway," Ashton told him. "You're in no state for it."

Blake meekly assented and allowed Ashton to drive them back to his cottage almost in silence. It was not until they were seated again by the fire which Ashton had replenished, drinking the hot tea which Ashton had busied himself to make, that he felt up to asking any questions.

"Ashton, for God's sake what *was* that thing?"

"Are you sure you want to talk about it now?" Ashton asked. "Wouldn't you like to just get off to bed and discuss it in the morning?"

"Thanks," Blake replied, adding with a wry smile, "I realize you're giving me the standard treatment for shock - warmth and hot tea - but I would like to talk about it. Nothing like that has ever happened to me before. The black dog - what was it?"

"As I said before," replied Ashton, "an elemental. A non-human entity. In this case, one evidently hostile to humanity and therefore what our ancestors would have called a demon."

"You dispelled it," Blake commented and looked at Ashton with a certain new-found respect. Ashton looked away as if disinclined to pursue this aspect of the matter.

"Well," he said, "one can't have studied the occult for years without learning a few things. But I think we have found the reason for its haunting of that particular spot. Remember that other thing we saw?"

"I do indeed." Blake's voice was low and he moved nearer to the blazing logs.

"There are many tales of haunted crossroads," Ashton continued. "So many, in fact, that such apparitions are sometimes called gibbet-ghosts. That is what we saw there, you know. A gibbet: the contrivance on which the remains of executed felons used to be hanged in chains, as a deterrent to others."

"You mean they were just left there?" Blake sounded incredulous.

"That's right," Ashton replied. "The bodies hung there, sometimes for years, until they fell to pieces and the remains were buried nearby, usually in a nameless grave. Often the gibbet would be raided in the dead of night by practitioners of black magic seeking human bones for use in their spells. The gibbet with its horrible burden was quite a well-known landmark in Merry England in the old days - right up to 1854 - when it was abolished by statute. The bodies of highwaymen in particular were treated in this way. They used to hang them at some legal place of execution like Tyburn Tree and then expose the body on a gibbet somewhere near the place where their crime was committed. The local blacksmith may have made that iron cage-like thing we saw - a set of gibbet-irons, they used to call it. Sometimes the poor devil was measured for it in prison, while he was still alive. The horror of such punishment excites pity, villains though most of such fellows were.

"You know, Blake, we are much inclined to romanticise the past. The reality of olden days was often squalid and hideous. The real-life highwaymen, smugglers and so on were savage and cruel men and so were the authorities that dealt with them. If some of our tourists could see the frightful deeds that really happened in what they regard as charming old-world places" He shivered slightly, gazing somberly into the fire.

"And were crossroads a favourite place for the gibbet?" Blake questioned.

"Yes, indeed. And for the burial of suicides and anyone who died in circumstances regarded as accursed.

With the traditional stake through the heart, too, to prevent them from becoming vampires. There is a crossroads not far from Lewes which is named to this day after a witch who was supposed to have been executed and buried there. It is no wonder that the vicinity of some old crossroads is often badly haunted. Such atmospheres attract dangerous elementals of the kind we saw. Well, it is very late, Blake, or rather very early into the small hours. You'd better get some rest."

"I think if you don't mind," said Blake, "I'd rather doze here by the fire until the dawn."

Ashton agreed; but Blake did not sleep until the first pale light arose over the heathland of Ditchling Common as the sun, the dispeller of phantoms, approached the horizon.

# The Old Oak Chest

*"The mistletoe hung in the castle hall.*
*The holly branch shone on the old oak wall.*
*And the Baron's retainers, blithe and gay,*
*Were keeping their Christmas holiday*
*Oh, the mistletoe bough!*
*Oh, the mistletoe bough!"*

Blake sang the old ballad vigorously and cheerfully, as he helped Ashton put up the Christmas decorations. It was a crisp, sunlit winter's morning of the day before Christmas and Blake was Ashton's unexpected though welcome guest. Blake usually spent Christmas at the home of his married elder brother; but this year a lamentable outbreak of measles had laid all three of the children low, so Blake thought it more tactful to postpone his visit. Instead, he had asked Ashton if he could possibly put him up.

"Don't put yourself out, though, if it's not convenient. I can always go to a hotel."

"Of course not," Ashton had replied over the telephone. "Don't go to any hotel. I'll be delighted to have you, though I'm afraid you may find it rather dull. I like a quiet, old-fashioned Christmas - the old decorations, the old music, a good lunch and then just sitting by the fire and listening to the Queen's speech. If that will suit you, come along."

Blake had replied that it would suit him splendidly, so here he was. He had found that what Ashton meant by the old decorations were the traditional branches and sprays of holly, mistletoe and dark evergreen box-leaves, intertwined with long trails of glossy-leaved ivy. All artificial paper-chains and so on were firmly banished. Moreover, no decorations were put up until Christmas Eve itself.

I don't keep the shopkeepers Christmas, which starts in September. I keep the good old Yuletide, Ashton had said. So putting up the decorations was now Blake's occupation, while Ashton polished old candlesticks and set bright red candles in them, to the accompaniment of Blake's voice singing of partridges in pear-trees and of the rising of the sun and the running of the deer.

An anticipatory glass or so of some excellent sherry might have contributed to Blake's vocal cheerfulness. At any rate Ashton, who was genuinely fond of music, suffered him for a while; but when he began the old ballad of the Mistletoe Bough Ashton turned away frowning.

Taking no notice, Blake continued the musical story of the young bride who had disappeared on her wedding day and whom the bridegroom and the guests had sought in vain, until years later the terrible solution of the mystery was found.

> *"At length an old chest that had long lain hid*
> *Was found in the castle - they raised the lid:*
> *And a skeleton form lay mouldering there,*
> *In the bridal wreath of the lady fair.*
> *Oh, sad was her fate! In sportive jest*
> *She hid from her lord in the old oak chest.*
> *It closed with a spring, and her bridal bloom*
> *Lay withering there in a living tomb.*
> *Oh, the mistletoe bough!*
> *Oh, the mistletoe bough!"*

Blake sang with a merriment quite inappropriate to this lugubrious tale, until Ashton burst out, " For God's sake, Blake, stop it! Sing anything but that!"

Blake fell silent and looked rather surprised. It was not like Ashton to be ill-tempered.

"I'm sorry, old chap. I suppose it is a pretty ghastly tale, really, when you come to think of it."

Ashton recovered himself and apologised. "No, it is I who should be sorry, Blake. The fact is, I can't stand that old song. It is, as you say, one of the grimmest of English folk-tales. There are several places where it is supposed to have happened. Bawdrip in Somerset and Owslebury in Hampshire are two of them. But it isn't that. It's what the song itself reminds me of. Something that happened years ago."

"Do I smell a story?" asked Blake, his good humour restored.

"Yes, if you would like to hear it," said Ashton. "And the least I can do, after snapping at you like that on a jolly Christmas Eve, is to tell it to you. Let's sit down by the fire and have a rest, while I think back to how it began."

"Well, it began with a villain I used to know. He was, to me, a particularly obnoxious villain, because he was the sort who brings my old profession of dealing in antiques into disrepute. He didn't look like a villain, of course; except that he was perhaps a shade too well-dressed. He called himself Delamere mostly, though I'm pretty certain that wasn't his real name. I believe he chose it because he thought it sounded aristocratic and looked well on business cards. He liked to try to pass himself off as being rather top-drawer - a characteristic which in practice is the almost certain hallmark of the guttersnipe, in my opinion. But anyway, I'll call him Delamere.

Delamere's specialty was conning elderly people into selling him their treasures at a fraction of their real worth. Once he had talked his way into some poor old soul's home, there was no getting rid of him. He could be glib, oily and persuasive; or he could change over to being domineering and bullying if he thought he could get away with it, until the old man (or more often the old lady) accepted his price just to get him out of the house.

Of course, the police knew Delamere and his business methods well. They had tried to nail him several times; but the old people concerned were usually so vague and confused that they were hopeless as witnesses, so the prosecution would fail because the case couldn't be proved.

The last of Delamere's victims was an old lady called Mrs. Chudleigh, somewhere in her eighties, whom Delamere obtained a number of valuable antiques from, in spite of her feeble protests that she didn't want to sell. In particular, I remember, he pressed twenty pounds on her for a beautiful Georgian table that he later sold for several hundreds. Mrs. Chudleigh realised that she had been victimised and went to the police; but Delamere as usual got off. The old lady told me afterwards, I know I was weak and foolish to sign that receipt; but I was so bothered and upset. "Oh, he knew how to keep just within the law all right - from long practice!' So Delamere left the court wearing that oily smile of his and Mrs. Chudleigh went away in tears. Case dismissed.

Now, Mrs. Chudleigh had a friend, a Miss Bishop, who was at least the same age as herself if not older. If you could have seen Miss Bishop, you would have called her a typical old-fashioned spinster. She was thin, grey haired, very upright and had remarkably bright and penetrating eyes. She was always what used to be called very lady-like in manner and appearance and both her house and her person were impeccably tidy.

Now, I had noticed this lady sitting at the back of the court on the occasion of the case concerning Mrs. Chudleigh. So I was surprised later to learn that Delamere had been invited by Miss Bishop to call on her with a view to purchasing some things, as she must have known, after the court case, what a villain he was. But this is anticipating the story.

What happened was that some while afterwards I got a letter from Miss Bishop, very neatly written upon her headed notepaper, telling me that she intended to move into a smaller and more labour-saving house as "she was not getting any younger, as the saying went." This meant that she would have to dispose of some of her furniture and antiques. She was kind enough to say that she would like me to have first choice. I accepted with alacrity, as I knew that a lady like Miss Bishop was likely to have some fine things. So we finalised the arrangements by telephone and one sunny afternoon I went round to see her.

She received me quite cordially and invited me to look over the house. It was a detached property in a quiet, good-class street. Everything was in perfect order; but I could see that it was rather a large residence for an elderly lady on her own. It was, perhaps, just a little on the dark side; but with the sunshine streaming through a window here and there, as it was today, the house was pleasant enough.

Most of the furniture was solid Victorian stuff, but of top quality and gleaming with polish. The pictures were older and really good - beautifully coloured prints, charming flower pieces and country scenes. There were some good vases, too; candlesticks and all sorts of small things - but I mustn't ramble on. You know how I feel about good antiques, apart from it being my profession.

One thing, though, caught my eye beyond all the rest. It was a splendid old oak chest, oblong and deep. Indeed, it must have been over six feet long and deep in proportion. I would say that it dated from at least the seventeenth century, if not before.

It was standing on a dim landing at an angle of the stairs; and I noticed it particularly because it was underneath a window with ornamental coloured glass in it, through which a beam of sunlight streamed that was full of dancing golden motes.

The old lady had gone to look for a portfolio of prints that seemed as if they might be of historic interest; so I took the liberty of going up the flight of stairs to examine the chest more closely. It proved to be richly carved with curious figures. There was a foliate mask - what we often call the Green Man, only this one had horns; there were the sun and moon and various creatures, including a goat, a cat, an owl and a hare. All around were sprays of leaves and flowers, especially oak leaves, while in the centre was a skull and crossed bones, surrounded by a wreath of poppies. There was another figure, too, that I couldn't quite make out; but it seemed to be someone muffled up in a cloak and hood.

It was a wonderful piece and I gazed at it fascinated, running my fingers instinctively over the smooth old wood. And then I began to have a very strange experience, one of the strangest of my life."

Ashton broke off his discourse and rose from his chair to fetch a large book from the bookcase. Blake, a little surprised at this sudden digression, watched him search for and find a certain page. Ashton held out the book and said, "Blake, I want you to look carefully at this picture."

The book was quite modern and one of what has come to be known as the coffee-table variety, from its size and the profusion of its coloured pictures. This particular volume dealt with witchcraft, demonology and magic. Blake found himself looking at a full-page coloured reproduction of a picture by an unknown master of the Flemish School, dating from the latter part of the fifteenth century.

It depicted a scene of witchcraft. In the centre, a young witch, naked save for a wisp of transparent drapery and a pair of curious pointed-toed sandals, was pouring a love-philtre upon the image of a human heart. The action was taking place in the witch's private room, with a fire burning in the grate and a pet dog, perhaps her familiar, curled up on a cushion. Just opening the door of the room, with an expression of entrancement upon his face, was a young man, presumably the object of her spell.

"It's a charming picture, in all senses of the word," Blake remarked. "But I don't quite see the relevance to what you've been saying."

"Whoever painted that picture, Blake, knew better than most what he was depicting-," Ashton replied. "Do you see those queer coiling shapes, like ribbons of light, that seem to be hanging in the air or floating about the room in the picture?"

"I do," Blake answered, rather puzzled.

"Well," Ashton continued, as he laid the book aside, "when I stood by that old chest, it *might* have been the dancing motes in the sunbeam which affected my eyes, but I seemed to see long silvery wisps of vapourish substance coming out from under the lid of the chest in ribbon-like streamers which coiled and floated in the air around me, just like the ones in that picture. I started to watch them in a bemused sort of way. And then it seemed as if a little thin silver voice started talking inside my head, persistently, monotonously, telling me to come and get inside the chest, it is just the right size, come, come and lie down in the dark, the peaceful dark, the shadows waiting for you, the kingdom of the shades, just raise the lid, lie down in the dark, the shadowy silent place is calling you, calling you, lie down, you must get inside and lie down and close the lid and it will be all dark, dark earth of death and spellbound silence, you are spellbound, spellbound - and the little deadly silvery voice went on and on and I had just begun to lift the lid, when I felt a touch on my arm and the spell was broken.

Miss Bishop had come up the stairs behind me and touched me rather sharply on the elbow, saying, 'No, Mr. Ashton. That chest is not for you.'

She *might* have meant simply that the chest was not for sale; but judging by subsequent events I'm not so sure.

What I looked like, goodness knows - dazed, to say the least of it. But Miss Bishop apparently noticed nothing unusual. She remarked brightly that looking over houses was tiring and she was sure I would like a nice cup of tea. Did I like Earl Grey tea? And she had some fresh homemade cakes.

So I followed her downstairs to the drawing room, where she plied me with tea and cakes, both of which were excellent and served from a delightful old willow pattern tea service. I soon recovered my composure, though inwardly I was very puzzled at my odd experience.

We completed our business transactions satisfactorily. I bought a number of good things from her and saw quite a few more that I would have liked to buy; but she wouldn't part with them and I didn't press her. I knew that she had let me have all that she was disposed to sell of the smaller and finer things. As for the heavy and less valuable stuff, that wasn't so much in my line, so I didn't mind when she said that she was calling in another dealer to get rid of that.

So I loaded my purchases carefully into my car and drove back to the shop. However, I was rather disconcerted the next day to discover that the other dealer involved was the odious Delamere - odious to me at any rate.

He came up to me in the street, smiling as usual and saying something about how nice it was that there were no ill feelings about the court case - in fact, Mrs. Chudleigh's neighbour, Miss Bishop, had invited him to her house that evening!

I made him some polite but brief answer and went on. The man knew I had no use for him, which was why he made a point of speaking to me. He was like that.

Thinking it over, I wondered if I should warn Miss Bishop. Yet I remembered that I had seen her in court when Delamere's case was heard. And Mrs. Chudleigh was her old friend - I couldn't understand it. And then - and then I thought again, recalling that queer happening when I stood beside the old oak chest. And I wondered if perhaps it was Delamere who should be warned; because I also remembered something else, just one little fact that lingered in my mind about Miss Bishop. But by this time Delamere was out of sight.

Indeed, I never saw him again. Over the next few days, it was eventually realised that Delamere had disappeared. He was neither at his shop nor at his home.

There was some speculation in the trade; but Delamere was a shady character and it was generally thought that he had chosen to disappear for some reason of his own.

Then Miss Bishop, neatly dressed as usual with immaculate light gloves and rolled umbrella, called at the police station. She was sorry to have to trouble them, but she was afraid there was something wrong. Mr. Delamere had called on her several days ago about buying some furniture and then - well, she hadn't seen him leave the house, he had just disappeared; and two Georgian silver snuff-boxes seemed to have disappeared with him.

The police recorded her statement with relish and acted on it promptly. As I told you, they had been trying to get Delamere for some time, but he had always been too sly for them. They went back with Miss Bishop to search the house and find out just how much was missing.

I had the details of what followed from one of the police officers whom I happened to know, over an off-duty drink. They couldn't see anything missing apart from the snuff-boxes; but eventually they got around to lifting the lid of the old oak chest. They took one look inside - and then the accompanying policewoman kindly but firmly led old Miss Bishop downstairs out of the way, while the officer in charge got on the 'phone to the station.

Inside the chest lay Delamere, dead for several days. He was stretched out on his back, with staring eyes and contorted features. A horrible sight, according to my policeman friend - a nasty way to go, even for a villain like Delamere. You see, the chest only opened from outside and it was very thick and heavy. A search of the dead man's pockets had revealed the two silver snuff-boxes.

The official police opinion was that Delamere had concealed himself in the chest in order to creep out later and rob the house, having scooped up the two snuffboxes from where they had been placed (rather temptingly, I thought) among some other oddments on a side table.

There was an inquest, of course; but Miss Bishop was spared as much as possible from giving evidence. The Coroner evidently regarded her as a somewhat confused old lady and warned her gently about being careful who she let into her home. The verdict was 'Misadventure'.

In no way, however, had Miss Bishop given me the impression of being confused. Nor could I forget my own strange experience in her house, which on reflection now coupled with that fact that I had remembered about her."

"What was that?" asked Blake as Ashton paused in his narrative.

"Well," Ashton replied after a moment's thought, "it was just that Miss Bishop had told me that her people came originally from near Wincanton in Somerset. Now, it might of course be mere coincidence. Bishop is quite a common name. But if you read old Joseph Glanvill who wrote about Somerset witchcraft in the seventeenth century, you will find that Ann Bishop was the name of a leading member of a Somerset witch coven in that area.

It has always been the tradition that witchcraft is handed down in families. I remember when I went to Jersey in the Channel Islands a few years back, being told that there were some old Jersey families who up until the eighteenth century at least and perhaps even later, secretly prided themselves on possessing 'le grand sang', meaning witches' blood, inherited from an ancestress who had been begotten at a witches' Sabbat. And you will find the story is everywhere the same. The old beliefs are there, too, just under the surface, if you know what to look for and where to look.

I kept my opinion to myself, of course, about these events; but the old lady has passed on now, so I feel that I can speak of it, to you at any rate."

"And what became of the chest?" asked Blake. "Did you ever get a chance to purchase it? It must have been a valuable piece."

"You are getting as keen on antiques as I am," replied Ashton with a smile. "But no, the chest never came up for sale.

Knowing its history, I'm not sure I should have wanted it if it had. Miss Bishop left it in her will to a favourite niece, who took it back to Somerset with her. I met the young lady briefly, a few years later, when she came here to settle up her aunt's affairs. A nice, refined country girl, very like Miss Bishop in her features. I noticed especially that she had just the same very steady, rather piercing eyes."

"So you think she might be ?" said Blake, with a quizzical look.

"Yes," said Ashton. "And I also think we'd better start preparing lunch."

Doreen Valiente

# The Quest Of The Book

"You know, Ashton, I'm really beginning to think that the place is bedevilled - literally!"

The speaker, Jeremy Blake, was lounging disconsolately in his friend Charles Ashton's kitchen, watching Ashton as the latter stood in apron and shirtsleeves polishing a silver tray. The informality of the scene was due to the fact that Blake's visit to Ashton's country cottage was unexpected and happened on the spur of the moment. As Blake had said, he was just fed up with the whole affair and didn't know what to do but drive over and ask Ashton's advice.

"You're perfectly welcome, old chap," Ashton had greeted him in response to his apologies. "I'm just doing some silver cleaning, but there's no hurry about it. Come into the kitchen and have a cup of tea and tell me what's bothering you."

So Blake sipped his tea and unfolded his tale of woe. "You see," he told Ashton, "it's this pair of old Victorian houses that my firm has got lumbered with. As you know, we do quite a bit in the way of reclaiming and rebuilding derelict properties. But it's usually business premises we deal with. We don't want to be bothered with residential property, it's too much hassle these days. However, these two old houses came to us as part of a larger deal and we're stuck with them.

They're ugly old places - a pair of semi-detached in a little back street in an old part of Brighton. Just two floors above (ground floor and upstairs, that is) and a basement. Both the houses are empty and rapidly falling into disrepair. However, with the price of house property what it is today, the firm felt that it might be possible and worth while to renovate them; and that's where I came in. I got the job of deciding whether to repair the houses or demolish them. They didn't look too bad to me, so I decided we could renovate. And that's when my troubles began!"

"What's the problem, then?" Ashton enquired, taking a seat at the kitchen table. "Have you got squatters?"

"Squatters? No," Blake replied. "But it's funny you should say that. Because we had squatters - and a rough-looking lot, too. But they moved out as quickly as they had moved in, or so I'm told. One of them was found wandering the streets in a state of shock and taken to hospital."

"Really?" Ashton commented. "You're sure it was shock and not drugs?"

"Well, he couldn't give any coherent account of himself; but the hospital was quite definite about the cause of his condition. They were suspicious that our firm had been using strong-arm methods to get rid of the squatters; but I can assure you it was nothing of the kind. I don't know why they bolted; any more than I know why the other people who were there before bolted too - and *they* were legitimate tenants!"

"That's odd," said Ashton. "People don't lightly give up tenancies these days, with housing so hard to find. Have you made any enquiries?"

"Well," Blake answered, "I've asked around the local pubs and shops to see what gossip I could pick up. It seems there are some queer stories circulating about these two old houses. One of them was last tenanted by an eccentric recluse, an unpleasant old man who had occupied one of the houses all by himself. He would never let anyone in and people round there where were afraid of him. In fact, it sounds to me as if he finally scared the people in the other house away. Apparently he'd been on bad terms with them for years and he was the sort of person it was better not to cross. I'm glad I haven't got to deal with him, from the stories I've heard."

"You mean he's gone, too?" asked Ashton in surprise.

"Yes - just disappeared." Blake laughed ruefully.

"You know, one woman I talked to, an old dear who keeps a little shop near there and assured me she was a good Catholic, quite seriously believed he was a Satanist and that the devil had come for his own!"

Ashton did not seem to think this was funny. "And what do you think?" he asked Blake.

"Well," Blake replied, "I *had* thought, up until now, that it was just a case of a lonely, eccentric old man, quite well-educated apparently in spite of his unkempt appearance (it seems he was an artist and quite a good one) and of people calling him a Satanist just because they didn't understand him. But after this afternoon - well, the whole thing's just rather got on my nerves."

"What happened this afternoon?" Ashton asked. By now he was keenly interested and was watching Blake closely.

"Well, it's what's been happening all the time, ever since I started on the job. Accidents, senseless rows over nothing - you could just about sum it up by saying that every damn thing that *could* go *wrong, did* go wrong. And this afternoon was the clincher. I'd put in a gang of three workmen, a foreman and two others, to start the work of renovation. They're three good chaps and I thought that by today we'd have the preliminary problems licked and could really get started. So I talked over what was to be done and then went back to the office and left them to it.

I went back to the site after lunch and found a crowd gathered and the police in possession! Hardly any progress had been made with the work, for several good reasons. Firstly, my foreman had fallen through a window and cut himself so badly that he had to be taken to hospital. Then after the ambulance had left, my two workmen had adjourned to the local pub for a prolonged lunch. They had come back fighting drunk and had been punching each other, shouting and swearing, until a disgusted local resident called the police. They were now standing, bloodied and sheepish-looking, while the sergeant gave them a ticking-off. I packed them off home, asked myself what the hell was the matter with this place and what the hell I was to do about it - and the only answer I came up with was to come and talk to you!"

"Had the workmen ever behaved like this before?" Ashton asked.

"Never!" Blake was quite emphatic. "That's what I can't understand. We've employed them for years. I won't say they're angels; but they've been normal, reliable fellows - up until now."

"And how about the atmosphere of the place? I mean the houses themselves?"

"Well," Blake responded after a moment's thought, "any derelict old house seems mournful and rather creepy, doesn't it? But - well, it may be my fancy, but I'd call this place menacing, somehow. I kept on getting the impression that there was someone watching me, just out of sight. In fact, I sort of jumped round, you know, a couple of times, half expecting to see some movement; but of course there was nothing there."

Ashton sat thoughtfully silent for a while, weighing up what Blake had told him. Then he rose from his chair, saying, "No, it's not your fancy, Blake. I've got a feeling about this business, in view of the details you've given me. I'd like to see the place for myself. Would you like to drive me over there now? I'll just put this stuff away quickly and get my coat. We've time to have a look round before dark."

Ashton took off his butler's apron and hung it on a peg, then quickly replaced his indoor shoes with a heavier pair and went in search of his favourite old Harris tweed jacket with leather patches on the elbows. Blake was both surprised and gratified at his friend's haste to investigate. Evidently he had succeeded in convincing Ashton that there was something seriously wrong. Or was Ashton's feeling based upon some psychic hunch? At any rate, he was glad to be driving back to Brighton with him, if only to get something done about a situation that had begun to worry him.

It was mid-afternoon when the car pulled up in the shabby Brighton back street where the pair of old houses was situated. Blake was glad it was a fine, sunny day; though even so there was something forbidding about the aspect of these dwellings. Peeling paint and broken windows could of course be remedied. Indeed, many old houses in these little side streets had been made quite charming. But decay seemed to have settled upon this place - a decay that was not only physical. You could imagine walking down here alone after dark and suddenly seeing something very nasty indeed peering at you from one of the windows. 'Pull yourself together', Blake told himself firmly. No point in imagining things like that. He produced the keys, unlocked the front door of one house and showed Ashton over it.

There was not a great deal to see, as neither house was very large nor apparently very remarkable. "This is the house the family lived in, isn't it?" Ashton asked.

"Yes, that's right. The old man lived next door," Blake replied, privately wondering how Ashton knew, as he couldn't recollect telling him. "As you see, it's very dirty and scruffy, but there's not much wrong with it structurally. The place next door is worse."

"Then let's see that, please," said Ashton, who up to now had looked shrewdly at everything but made little comment.

They ascended the stairs from the dingy basement and returned to the narrow hall and the outside world. Then Blake locked the door behind them and proceeded to unlock the door of the second house.

Ashton sniffed the air that met them as they entered the dark little hallway. "Have you noticed it, Blake?" he asked. "Even the air through the broken windows has not dispersed it."

"Dispersed what? Both of these houses smell - well, they smell like old houses!" Blake tried to lighten the atmosphere with a laugh.

"This one smells different," said Ashton. "It smells very faintly of incense - a certain very peculiar incense." He paused for a few moments, then proceeded towards the basement.

"The smell is stronger down there," said Blake. "But you'll find the place is absolutely bare."

Indeed, it proved to be so, apart from the scattered debris left by the workmen's abortive efforts.

"What happened to the old man's possessions?" asked Ashton.

"Well, there was nothing here but a lot of old junk," Blake replied. "We gathered it all up and stowed it in the bedroom. Just in case he ever came back, you know; but I don't think he will."

"How about his pictures? I understand he was supposed to be an artist."

"We found a few rough paintings on hardboard - looked like sketches for larger works; but that's all. They're upstairs, too. Very well done, but I wouldn't want them on my walls. His favourite subjects, apparently, were scenes of black magic and torture. There's one really vile thing of two old hags digging up a corpse, while their demon familiar looks on. And there's another of a moonlit wood and a man half-way changed into a wolf - you can guess the sort of stuff. But none of it's worth calling a finished picture."

"I want to see this, Blake, if you please," Ashton requested after a thoughtful pause. "The influence of evil is strong in this basement; but the essential clue I am looking for seems to be elsewhere."

The two men left the basement and mounted the uncarpeted stairs, their footsteps echoing through the old house. Blake noticed uneasily that the afternoon sun was beginning to fade. He opened the door of the bedroom and displayed a crowded jumble of frowsy old furniture, cooking pots, old clothes, old tubes of paint and miscellaneous rubbish. Ashton looked it over briefly, giving most attention to a scrutiny of the unframed sketches Blake had described. Then he moved around the room with one hand outstretched, as if divining for something. He stopped before a small cupboard on the wall beside the fireplace.

"This is it, Blake! There is something here. We must have it open."

The cupboard was locked and the key missing; but Blake hastened to find a large screwdriver and the flimsy door soon yielded. He jumped back as it swung open, half expecting something horrible to fall out towards him. But he was immediately conscious of an acute sense of anticlimax. The cupboard was empty.

No, wait a moment - it had been too dark in the shadow for him to see. There was a folded sheet of paper on the shelf. Blake drew it out. Just a dirty, yellowed sheet of cheap typing paper, with some lines of typing on it, done by an unskilled hand upon an old machine. It seemed to be some sort of poem. He read out the title by the fading sunset light that filled the room, 'To the *Necronomicon*'.

"Ashton, what on earth is the *Necronomicon*?"

"Nothing on earth," replied Ashton gravely. "Elsewhere I am not so sure. It was written about in the 1930s by an American author of weird tales named Howard Phillips Lovecraft. The *Necronomicon* is a grimoire - or perhaps I should say *the* grimoire, the ultimate source-book of black magic."

"Ah, now I remember!" Blake exclaimed. "Of course; I think I've read some of his stuff, years ago. But it's just fiction, isn't it? I mean, there never was such a book as the *Necronomicon*. It's just an invention of Lovecraft's. And this ties up, now I come to think of it, with something else I heard in the pub gossip about the old recluse. Apparently he was supposed to have spent most of his life in searching for a certain very rare book. It would be rather pathetic, wouldn't it, if it was a book that didn't exist?"

Ashton paused for a moment before replying. Then he said, "Some occult scholars now believe that Lovecraft may have had access to certain arcane lore, upon which his fantasies were based. Some of them, for instance, tie up with passages in Madame Blavatsky's monumental work, *The Secret Doctrine*. But the light is fading, Blake. We had better read this paper while we still can."

Taking the paper from Blake's outstretched hand, Ashton began to read its contents aloud:

*"To the Necronomicon*

*Thou mystic volume of forbidden lore,*
*Writ by Alhazred's trembling hand of yore,*
*Where dost thou hide? What nameless guardian*
*Witholds thy pages from the eyes of man?*
*In some black lightless crypt art thou inhumed.*
*That is by naught but spiders eyes illumed?*
*What mummied hand doth hold thee in its grasp,*
*Where dust of ages films thy jewelled clasp?*
*Or art thou locked in secret sanctuary*
*Where none but the initiate may see,*
*Where silent robed priests the scrolls unfold*
*From carven chests of ebony and gold*
*In Schamballah, deep in Agharti's fane.*
*Which snow-clad summits guard from the profane;*
*So that our learning, fragmented and brief.*
*Hears but the whispered name of Al Azif?*
*The Lords of Silence - deemed they better so.*
*That this the outer world should little know*
*Of all thy secrets, monstrous and malign,*
*Or the dark splendours that thou dost enshrine?*
*And yet, across the regions desolate.*
*The wandering winds may wail about thy gate,*
*With fleshless fingers plucking at the door*
*To hidden places sealed an age before,*
*Shunned with stark fear by travellers that wend*
*Those lonely ways, and long for journey's end,*

*Crowding about the camp-fire's fitful light*
*That shields them from the demon-haunted night.*
*Or mouldering in some ancient castle's hall,*
*Is there a shelf that none doth now recall,*
*Upon it an old book, close-locked and grim,*
*Lit by a gleam through windows rich and dim,*
*Bound with an eldritch magic seal unknown.*
*That some strange wizard ancestor did own?*
*Fearful and yet desired; O magic tome.*
*In some dark catacomb, what grinning gnome*
*Crouches by thee? And by the light of day*
*Would thine abhorred letters melt away.*
*Crumbling to dust? No, thou too dost partake*
*Of that fell verse the Arab sage did make:*
*That is not dead which can eternal lie;*
*And with strange aeons, even death may die."*

As Ashton's voice died away, the two men stood for a moment in silence, while the shadows grew thicker around them in the deserted house. Then Ashton folded the paper again and replaced it in the cupboard, saying, "We had better be going, Blake."

"Take the poem with you if you like," Blake invited him. "No, thanks," was the response. "I've learned all I can for the moment. I don't particularly want that thing in my house. And if I were you, Blake, I would leave it where it is."

The two men made their way down the stairs and out into the street, where the car was waiting. Blake locked the door behind them and thankfully got into the car to drive Ashton home.

Ashton was very quiet and seemed lost in thought. Eventually, Blake enquired, Well, what do you make of it?"

"I cannot see the whole picture yet," was the reply. "But I am certain from what I felt in the atmosphere of that place that we are up against something very serious here. Blake, will you excuse me if I don't ask you to stay to dinner? I want to do some occult work of my own tonight, in that little private room of mine that you know of. I hope it may help towards the solution of this affair."

Blake acquiesced in Ashton's wishes, as he realised Ashton would be working to help him. He had seen Ashton's private study, with its heavily curtained windows and shelves of his rarest books. Blake was one of the few people who knew that the study also served as a private magical temple; though an initiate might have deduced as much from the large and intricatepainting of the Qabalistic 'Tree of Life', done by Ashton himself, which hung upon one wall.

Accordingly, the two friends parted at Ashton's gate. But before Blake left, Ashton said to him, "Get your workmen to carry on as best they can at that place. I think you may find things a little better after tonight. But don't take any chances. And give me a ring right away if you discover anything else, or if anything of significance happens."

What was the nature of Ashton's magical working that night he did not confide to Blake. However, over the next couple of days things at the site seemed to go better. The atmosphere seemed somehow less tense and depressing. The two workmen, in the absence of their foreman who was still off sick on account of his injuries, willingly did what they could under Blake's direction. Indeed, they seemed anxious to make up for their previous misbehaviour and get back into his good graces. But without the foreman's skilled advice, activity was mainly confined to clearing out the rubbish. Blake took the opportunity to make a bonfire of the hideous pictures and felt somehow better for doing so.

He had been to see the foreman in hospital and learned that he was coming along well and expected to be discharged soon; but the man absolutely insisted that his fall was the result of a violent push from someone or something which crept up behind him. Moreover, he knew it was neither of the workmen who did it, because they were nowhere near at the time. Remembering this, Blake moved about the place with a certain circumspection.

However, nothing untoward happened and Blake began to think that perhaps the jinx was broken. The foreman left hospital and returned to work, or at any rate to light duties and general supervision. This enabled a start to be made on the essential work of renovation, beginning with a good look at the foundations, drains, etc., via the basement.

The next day Ashton's telephone shrilled out its summons and Blake's voice came excitedly on the line.

"Ashton, you know you asked me to call you about those old houses - if anything else happened, I mean?

Well, something has! We've found some sort of tunnel - and we've come to another dead stop. The workmen took one look at it and flatly refused to go on. Can't say I blame them, either, after what we know about the place.

To speak the truth, I'm scared of it myself. So I've fobbed them off with a yarn about getting in expert advice and sent them away to another job - to which they've gone very willingly."

"Where is this tunnel?" Ashton enquired.

"It's in the basement of the old man's house. You know, where you could smell that whiff of some strange incense. No wonder - the stench of it came welling out as soon as we forced the door. I think that's what upset the workmen - that, and the sinister look of that black hole."

"You say there was a door?" Ashton asked. "What sort of a door? Was it sealed?"

"Well, it was locked," Blake answered. "We thought it was a cupboard door until we got it open. But it's a passage, seeming to lead right into the earth."

"Well, you know, it could be connected with the old smuggling days," Ashton suggested. "When Brighton was the fishing village of Brighthelmstone, there was plenty of that going on. All sorts of odd passages and secret rooms have been discovered beneath Brighton's old buildings, especially near the sea. They've generally had to be bricked up because they'd become unsafe with the passing of time. They would be either escape routes when the customs men were about, or places to store contraband, or both. Your tunnel probably has another exit somewhere, perhaps in a neighbouring garden; and from what I've seen of these places before, it might well widen out below to make an underground room. There might even be a whole labyrinth of tunnels down there."

"I don't like the sound of that," said Blake uneasily. "This one looks quite scary enough for me. And what about the smell of incense?"

"I should think", said Ashton, "that the old man found this place and has been using it for his own purposes. If so, it would not be the first time that black magic has been practiced in the tunnels and crypts beneath old Brighton. There have been stories going back for many years. Have you been inside the tunnel yet, Blake?"

"Not likely!" Blake responded.

"Then don't. You have done the right thing in sending the workmen away. Lock the house up for now and we'll go down together tomorrow."

The next day, to Blake's relief, dawned clear and bright. Had it been dark and melancholy, he might have found it hard to nerve himself to go into that gloomy basement and explore whatever lay beyond it. But the sun shone cheerfully upon the familiar countryside as he drove over to collect Ashton according to their arrangement.

He found Ashton quite calm and cheerful also and dressed in what, for him, was an unusually colourful manner. Instead of his usual plain white or cream- coloured shirt and silk tie, Ashton was wearing a high- necked black sweater against which gleamed a large silver pendant set with turquoise stones. Many young men wore such things these days; but Blake had never seen Ashton in anything so trendy and he remarked on it.

Ashton smiled. "It is a very convenient fashion," he said. "It enables me to wear the old lama's gift without the attention that such a thing would have attracted years ago. Moreover, one of the pockets in this other garment - I believe they call it a safari jacket - will carry something else which I mean to take with me."

With these words, Ashton indicated a light brown tweed jacket of the kind described, hanging over a chair.

He proceeded to put the jacket on and Blake could see that there was indeed a slight bulge in the right-hand pocket.

"You're not taking a gun with you, surely?" Blake exclaimed.

"No," Ashton replied. "But it is a weapon just the same. It is a Tibetan *phurba*, or what ignorant Westerners have sometimes called a devil-dagger."

He produced the object from his pocket and showed it to Blake, but without allowing Blake to handle it. Blake saw that it was made of bronze and appeared to be very old. It had a curious blunt triangular blade and a hilt intricately fashioned to incorporate what seemed to be various god-like faces and other symbols, the meanings of which were unknown to him. He noticed that the hilt was also studded here and there with turquoise stones worked into the design.

"You said something about an old lama's gift?" Blake queried, looking intently at the strange weapon.

"That's right," Ashton answered, returning the devil-dagger to the concealment of his pocket. "Many years ago, when I was travelling in the East, I happened to be of some service to an old Tibetan lama who was a refugee from the Communist invasion of his country. He gave me these things in return - the *phurba* and several protective talismans, of which this I am wearing is one. You see, Blake, it is actually a sort of locket. Inside is a scrap of Tibetan paper with a *mantra* - that is, a sort of magical formula - written upon it. I have a similar one here for you and I am going to ask you to be good enough to wear it."

Blake eyed the heavy silver chain and turquoise-encrusted pendant dubiously. "Well," he said, "I suppose my jacket will hide it more or less. Thank goodness I shan't have to stop anywhere for petrol!"

He put the talisman round his neck, wondering as he did so about the age and history of this object from a far-away land.

"I didn't know you were involved with Tibetan things, Ashton," he remarked. "I've heard a lot about the supposed mystic powers of these Tibetan lamas, of course; but they didn't do much to save their own country, did they?"

"The Ancient Wisdom is basically the same all over the world," Ashton replied. "It just receives a different colouring according to the time and place in which it is found. As for the invasion of Tibet, it might surprise you to know that it was prophesied in detail, years before it happened, by one of the Dalai Lamas - the one they called the Great Thirteenth. He died in 1935; and not long before his death he wrote in his own hand a small book, just nine pages long, containing the prophecy and urging the Tibetan people to arm themselves and prepare to resist the invasion. But the idea of military resistance was profoundly repugnant to devout Buddhists and the Dalai Lama's dying prophecy went largely unheeded. We all know the results; and it would take a wiser man than I am to pronounce upon the working out of destiny, or *karma* as the people of the East call it.

My old Tibetan friend talked to me about these things; and he, too, was a prophet in his own way, because he foretold that one day I should have a special need of these consecrated objects that he gave me. Blake, I have a feeling that the time of that need is now. I don't quite know what I am up against in this case. That is why I am using this Tibetan magic. Shall we go?"

As he spoke, Ashton picked up from the floor an oil-filled hurricane lamp which had evidently been placed there in readiness.

"Don't you have an electric torch?" asked Blake.

"Yes, but I prefer this for the moment," was the reply. Blake guessed that Ashton had some reason for his choice, so he made no argument and the two men set off in Blake's car for Brighton.

They arrived at the quiet back street where the pair of old houses was situated and found everything apparently undisturbed. Blake took Ashton straight to the basement where the entrance to the tunnel had been discovered. Ashton held up his lighted lamp and surveyed the black opening behind the facade of a cheap, ordinary cupboard door without comment.

Blake flashed the light of his electric torch into the darkness and saw that some attempt had been made to shore up the tunnel with wooden props. They looked as if they had been there for a long time and he recalled Ashton's surmise about smugglers.

This surmise was turned to certainty as they penetrated further along the narrow passage. It broadened out into a fair-sized cellar which was piled high with the remains of old casks and boxes. Some of the wood still retained a faint aroma of brandy, mingling with the scent of that heavy incense which permeated the whole place.

The casks and boxes, most of them broken, had been piled against the walls to clear a space in the middle of the floor. Blake shone his torch on this and saw that a double circle had been painted upon the flagstones with red paint. Around it were inscribed various strange signs which he presumed were magical sigils.

The air seemed fairly fresh apart from the mingled scents which permeated the cellar. Blake guessed that there must be some other ventilation passage. The old-time smugglers had been very ingenious in their arrangements, he recalled, as many an old Sussex inn or farmhouse could testify.

Then he flashed his torch around the walls beyond the circle and gasped. For a moment he felt such a shock of terror that he almost fled back out of the cellar. Then he realised that the demon forms his torch had illuminated were paintings. Here at last was the recluse artist's finished work.

Frightful, unearthly figures writhed and glared from every vacant patch of whitewashed wall, interspersed with unknown hieroglyphics as if of some alien language. There were degenerate distortions of humanity mingled with nameless monsters of nightmare. The demons of hideous fantasy that haunted the darkest depths of the human mind snarled and grinned from those walls, painted by the hand of a depraved genius.

For a moment, Blake's hand that was holding the torch trembled as he stood speechless before the malign power of those paintings. Then Ashton held up the steadier glow of the hurricane lamp.

"An inspired artist, Blake," he said softly. "But from what realms did his inspiration come?"

He advanced firmly across the circle, with Blake following closely behind him, in order to inspect the further wall. The whitewash on this looked fresher, as if it had been more recently applied, especially to the central area. Had a further tunnel been closed? Or perhaps merely disguised? The same thought occurred to both men and they examined the wall closely.

Upon the newer surface was a peculiar design, quite different from anything else depicted in that fearsome place and apparently more innocent. Drawn in a dull brownish-red pigment was a large, roughly circular maze, somewhat resembling those featured upon the ancient coins of Cnossos. But what was the pigment? Not mere paint, like the circle on the floor. An unpleasant suspicion arose in Blake's mind that it was dried blood, or some other substances compounded with blood.

His eyes followed the windings of the maze; and then, he knew not why, he reached out and touched it and began slowly tracing its coiling path with his finger.

"Leave it alone, Blake!" whispered Ashton urgently; but Blake did not seem to hear him. He continued tracing the windings of the maze. Quite suddenly the temperature seemed to drop. An icy cold air pervaded the cellar, accompanied by a sibilant high-pitched sound like the stridulation of some gigantic insect.

Ashton forcibly pulled Blake backwards to the centre of the circle. Then they both gazed in horror at the maze. It had begun to glow with a greenish fire which pulsated as if with a life of its own. Blake cried out incoherently as he glimpsed another movement upon the walls. The monsters - the demons - they were coming alive!

Yes, here was movement of a sinuous tentacle, half-materialised! And there - there, surely, malignant eyes rolled, a frightful head turned, foul and abominable shapes loomed from the painted surface!

Blake strove desperately to keep his head and fight down panic. But he was almost overcome when the wall behind the maze seemed to disappear. In its place was a dark infinitude, as if of the spaces between the stars. Out of this, through the glowing, pulsating web of the maze, a figure began to appear, until it stood seemingly solid before the wall, with the maze behind it forming an aura of green luminescence like that of the creatures which glide in the unknown depths of the sea, where drowned Atlantis lies.

The figure was that of an old man wearing a hooded black robe. His face wore a grin of triumphant evil and in his arms was clutched a huge book. It was bound in the green and scaly skin of some great reptile and ornamented with curiously worked clasps of bronze.

Then, as if this was the climax for which he had been waiting, Ashton drew from his pocket that strange ancient dagger that had been the old lama's gift. He stepped forward and pointed it firmly at the black-robed figure, intoning as he did so the great mantra of the age-old wisdom of the East:

"OM MANI PADME HUM!
OM MANI PADME HUM!
OM MANI PADME HUM!"

Again and again Ashton repeated the chant, until that awful sound which was just on the borderline of normal hearing died away, the paintings were again nothing but ghastly painted forms and the green fire of the maze began to waver and grow dimmer.

Ashton made a sign in the air with the dagger and spoke in a tone of command, "In the name of all the Powers of Light, begone unto your own place and trouble us no more!"

The face of the black-robed apparition seemed contorted with fury; but it cowered back from the point of the *phurba*. Again Ashton began to intone the *mantra*, glancing sidelong at Blake as he did so to see how the younger man was holding up. Blake looked to be on the point of collapse and Ashton knew that the situation was dangerous. He was facing the strongest force of evil he had ever encountered. He could hold it at bay; but how could he get Blake safely out of there and seal the door against it?

"Have you got your torch, Blake?" he whispered. "Good - keep hold of it firmly and prepare to lead us out of here."

Blake tried to speak and his teeth chattered; but he took a deep breath, got a grip on himself and backed towards the entrance as Ashton lingered between him and that baleful black-robed phantom which grasped the great book.

As Ashton too backed away, still holding the *phurba* defensively, the maze glowed brighter and the apparition advanced out of the wall. Then Ashton suddenly flung the lighted lamp straight at it. The lamp went clean through the spectral form and the glass smashed against the painted wall. Burning oil flared up in a blaze.

"Out, Blake, quickly!" Ashton cried. With the aid of Blake's torch, the two men fled out of the cellar as clouds of smoke billowed after them. They heard the crackling of a fierce fire behind them, which had seized rapidly upon the old brandy casks and was soon licking at the dry wood that supported the tunnel.

"Purification by fire, Blake!" Ashton gasped as they paused for breath in the daylight above; light that they were profoundly glad to see.

It was evident that the whole place was going up in flames. They could do nothing but jump into Blake's car and move quickly out of danger. There was a bad moment when the car stalled; but fortunately it was due to nothing more than Blake's understandably shaky driving.

"Pull up at the first telephone box you see and call the fire brigade," said Ashton. "We'll have to do that, but you need only say there's been an accident with a lamp."

Privately, he was not sorry that by the time the brigade arrived the house was past saving. There would be questions to answer, of course. But Blake could handle it. And fire, the sacred element most near to spirit, would indeed cleanse that accursed place. Sitting in Blake's car, he watched the firemen and allowed himself to relax.

There were indeed questions to answer; but as Ashton had guessed, Blake was experienced in handling local authorities and as no insurance claim was involved, the matter passed off with no more than a rebuke from the fire brigade about the unwisdom of being careless with oil lamps in old houses. The house where that strange recluse and evilly talented artist had lived was a blackened shell, nor was the adjacent house much better. Demolition was the obvious course. As to what had really happened, that was something that Blake and Ashton discussed with no one but each other.

They were engaged in doing this by Ashton's fireside a couple of days later. Both still felt a reaction from the stress of what they had witnessed in that crypt which had been literally a hell-hole. But normality was returning and they even managed a laugh about the way in which Blake had remembered just in time to take off the Tibetan necklace and hide it in his pocket before speaking to the firemen.

"You showed great courage and presence of mind throughout, Blake," Ashton remarked. "I can tell you now that if you had lost your head - well, it might have been all up with both of us."

"But what was the meaning of it all, Ashton?" Blake asked. "That book - somehow it seemed to me to be the power-centre of the whole business. And yet you told me the *Necronomicon* doesn't exist."

"I said it didn't exist *in this world*," Ashton replied gravely. "But this is not the only world, Blake; merely the one our five senses are usually aware of. There are other dimensions and other entities which inhabit them, some glorious and some hideous. That man found a way of entering those other dimensions; but because of his own nature he chose the world of twilight and evil that occultists call the Lower Astral Plane. You remember he was obsessed with the search for the *Necronomicon*? Well, I think that when he failed to find it on earth he got the idea of opening a door to search for it in the beyond. And I think, Blake, that he may have found it. Just how, I do not know. It may be that Lovecraft was unconsciously transcribing from an original that exists in that world. Or it may be that the concentrated thought of the many occultists who have dreamed about the *Necronomicon* and visualised it has created a powerful thought-form that has become a reality upon its own plane. We talk easily about the power of thought, Blake; but only people like my old Tibetan lama fully understand what that implies. One thing, though, is certain. That door that was opened must be shut and *sealed*, before anyone else strays there and before anything more from that world strays into this one."

"How are we to do that?" Blake asked.

"I will consecrate a talisman," Ashton replied.

"You see, the evil of that place has been held at bay for the moment; long enough, I think, for you to send your bulldozers in to level the site. But before a clean, new dwelling is erected upon that ground we will bury the talisman in the earth. I'll need the co-operation of your foreman, Blake, to ensure that it is undisturbed.

Can you arrange that?"

"Oh, I think so," Blake answered. "Remember, he is the chap who was pushed through a window by something invisible. And he can be trusted to keep his mouth shut, too. I'll have a private talk with him."

Thus it came to be that early one sunlit morning after the site was cleared and leveled, Blake and Ashton arrived there before the workmen. Blake bore a spade and Ashton a small metal box, carefully sealed.

On the spot where, by prior secret agreement with the foreman, the talisman was to be buried, Blake dug a deep hole. The box was duly concealed within it and the hole filled in. Over it would be laid at least four inches of concrete, known in the building trade as the oversight. This in turn would be covered by the damp course of the new premises. "But won't the box eventually corrode and disintegrate?" Blake had objected. "No matter," was Ashton's reply. "What it contains is an engraved stone." Nor would he give any more precise description of it or of the ceremony of its consecration.

When the task of burying the talisman was completed and the spade stowed away in the car, Blake and Ashton strolled down to the seafront. They stood for a while leaning upon the railings of the promenade and gazing thoughtfully out to sea. The fresh morning sunlight sparkled upon the waves and seagulls soared and cried overhead.

"Well, Blake," said Ashton, "we have done all we can. And we may have closed a gate upon a great danger, not only to this place but to the soul of this country and perhaps even to the whole world."

"You know, Ashton," Blake remarked rather diffidently, "there's something I want to ask you. When you insisted on bringing that oil lamp, did you intend then to use it in the way you did?"

Ashton remained silent for a short while. When he eventually spoke, it was with a twinkle in his eye.

Well, if I did, Blake, I am technically guilty of arson! So I had better not answer your question directly in case I make you an accessory! But I think you know me well enough to believe that I had hoped such a measure would not be necessary and that I only resorted to it - if indeed I did - in the gravest circumstances. But it is all over now, I trust, so we will talk of it no more. Let's go and see if there is a decent cafe open yet - where we can get some breakfast."

The two men strolled along the sunlit promenade, as the voices of laughing children were borne towards them upon the fresh breeze. Groups of holiday-makers were beginning to fill the beach, all oblivious of the strange dramas that are sometimes secretly enacted in the hidden places of this world.

# The Witch-Ball Reappears

"I'm sorry to hear your husband's not been well, Mrs. Henderson. What's wrong?"

Charles Ashton looked around the usually neat little antique shop in a small Sussex town with some concern. To his experienced eye, there were signs of neglect which were unusual for his old acquaintances, the Hendersons, the elderly couple who ran it. There seemed to be less in stock than usual and what there was appeared dusty and ill-displayed. Mrs. Henderson looked careworn and apprehensive.

"Jack's just come out of hospital," she answered. "He's in the sitting-room. Do come in. It would cheer him up to see you."

Ashton followed her into the living quarters behind the shop, where he found Henderson sitting in an armchair by the fire. Ashton was shocked at his old friend's appearance. The man seemed to have aged ten years in the few months since Ashton's last visit.

"Well, old chap, what's been happening?" Ashton enquired with a cheerfulness, which masked his anxiety. He seated himself in the opposite armchair and prepared to listen to Henderson's troubles, which were evidently of a serious nature.

"I've been worked over," Henderson stated, managing to summon up a shaky smile. "Two young thugs nearly kicked me to death."

"What? Good Lord, what was it - robbery?"

"Not exactly, though it started with a robbery. Well, really, it all started with that damned witch-ball. I felt there was something uncanny about it somehow, when I first got the thing in the shop. And it's certainly brought me ill luck."

"A witch-ball?" Ashton queried. "Where is it now? I'd like to see that." He felt the stirring of a kind of premonition.

"Gone," Henderson replied. "And good riddance, perhaps; although I resent letting myself be robbed. But you'd have been interested to see it all right. It had passed through your hands in the old days, before you retired."

Ashton was now keenly interested. "Did you by any chance get it from - ?" And he named the wealthy show-business couple to whom, long ago, he had sold a certain ill-omened antique, the story of which he had told to Jeremy Blake on the occasion of their first meeting.

"It did come from their London flat, yes. Apparently a lot of their stuff was put in store when they split up. Eventually it was disposed of at a sale; and I happened to hear that they'd bought this particular thing originally from you."

At this juncture Mrs. Henderson came in with a tray of tea and buttered scones. "Do have some," she urged Ashton. "It will encourage Jack to eat."

Ashton readily complied and praised her home-made jam. Inwardly, he was deeply curious as to the further adventures of the haunted witch-ball; but he had no intention for the moment of telling Henderson all he knew.

Eventually, Ashton's kindly but probing questions elicited the full story. Henderson had bought the witch-ball and put it on display in his shop. One day, a young man in a black cloak had entered the shop, accompanied by several other strangely dressed people whom Henderson had vaguely classified as 'hippies'. They had looked at various articles and kept him talking, but eventually all left together without buying anything. As soon as they had gone, Henderson realised that the witch-ball had gone with them, probably concealed under the young man's cloak. He ran into the street after them, but was too late to catch them. However, he had recognised the black-cloaked individual and promptly telephoned the police.

He named the suspect as one Nicholas Dee, otherwise known as Master Nicholas. This was a young man who had several times got his name into the papers by claiming to be a local coven leader of great and mysterious powers and an expert on black magic. Henderson had recognised him from various dramatically posed photographs which had accompanied the newspaper articles. These had caused quite a bit of gossip in the small town; and from what Henderson had heard, he considered Master Nicholas to be a charlatan who was dealing in drugs and exploiting silly young girls. Dee claimed to be a descendant of the famous Elizabethan magus, Dr. John Dee; a claim which was probably as bogus as the rest of his set-up.

The police had duly gone looking for Master Nicholas; but he was nowhere to be found. When they eventually discovered his current address, at a derelict house which had been turned into a so-called 'commune', the place was quite clean of anything incriminating though filthy otherwise. Obviously a call from the police had been expected. There was nothing there but a heap of dog-eared paperback books about black magic, a lingering smell of cheap joss-sticks and cannabis and a motley collection of layabouts who jeered and giggled at the police officers carrying out the search. No one, of course, knew where 'The Master' had gone or anything about any theft from Henderson's shop.

However, a few nights later Henderson had been followed by two young roughs in jeans and black leather jackets. They had suddenly set upon him, punched him several times and then 'put the boot in' as he fell to the pavement. A passer-by found him lying there semi-conscious and covered in blood and called an ambulance.

While he was detained in hospital, Mrs. Henderson had been alone in the living-quarters of the shop. One night the telephone rang. An anonymous threatening voice spelled out to her in obscene detail just what would happen to her and her husband if he persisted in his complaint against 'The Master'.

On the first night after Henderson was discharged, the call was repeated. This time they both listened to it. The next day, Henderson wrote a letter to the police saying that he had been mistaken in his identification of Nicholas Dee and wanted to withdraw the charge.

Two police officers had called on him and tried to persuade him to change his mind; but Henderson refused and there was nothing more to be done. As he told Ashton, 'It's just not worth it. I can't take any more and neither can my wife. We're both of us getting on in years and I haven't been able to do much since it happened. All we want now is to put it behind us and forget it.'

Ashton listened sympathetically to Henderson's story and then insisted on giving Mrs. Henderson a hand to set the shop in order. As he dusted and polished, he thought furiously; for Ashton was not a man to lie down under injustice.

Nor was Jeremy Blake, to whom Ashton confided this narrative later with a view to enlisting his help. "This isn't quite our usual thing, Blake," he remarked. "There could be a bit of strong-arm stuff involved, if you and I take this business up."

"That's all right with me," was Blake's cheerful reply. "And if we need a bit of extra muscle, there are a couple of rugby football-playing hearties in my office who would love to join in."

Ashton smiled, saying, "Well, I hope it won't come to that. The Bulldog Drummond stuff went out of date with the 1930s. But I'll bear your offer in mind, though I'd prefer to try a more subtle approach to the problem first."

"You're determined to get the witch-ball back, then?" Blake queried.

"I feel it's my duty to get it back," Ashton replied, speaking more gravely. "You see, I can't deny to myself that this whole affair is my fault. I reproach myself strongly for it. I should never have allowed that thing to go out of my possession without taking steps to banish the evil that was associated with it. I was younger then and knew less about the occult than I do now; but even so, I should have done something."

Knowing Ashton's strong belief in the working-out of *karma* and its effect on the destiny of individuals, for good or ill, Blake offered no contradiction. Instead, he asked, "What about Master Nicholas?"

"Ah, yes," Ashton responded. "I intend to take cognisance of Master Nicholas, whatever happens to the witch-ball. You know, serious occultists usually ignore people like him. Some of us even think, perhaps rather cynically, that people like him have their uses in distracting the attention of the popular press from the real thing. But Master Nicholas is going a bit too far and getting a bit too nasty. Besides, there is always the chance that these would-be black magicians might manage to stir up something really evil and bring it through, into this world."

Remembering a certain previous adventure he had shared with Ashton and the horror they had faced together in the cellar of an old house, Blake went cold. He realised that there might be factors in this situation that would make it wise to leave Ashton to plan the campaign. However, before he left the comfort of Ashton's cottage that night to drive home to Brighton, he got Ashton to promise that the older man would not pursue any physically dangerous enquiries without him as a bodyguard.

A few days later Blake received a telephone call from Ashton to his Brighton flat. He listened as Ashton told him of a conversation with an acquaintance who worked for a local newspaper.

"This chap told me there have been a number of incidents of thefts from churches, graveyard desecration and so on in that area, that were strongly suspected to have some connection with black magic. But there was no evidence to bring a charge against anyone and the facts were sometimes hushed up because the vicar of the church concerned didn't want the sensational press to write it up. There's a big element of bravado in this sort of thing, you know, so it was probably a wise decision."

"And you think Master Nicholas and his lot were responsible for these incidents?"

"Oh, yes, very probably. It's one of the ploys of charlatans like him to set a new recruit to the black coven to do something like this for a dare, to prove themselves so to speak. What the newcomer doesn't realise is that he or she is being induced to commit a crime and to provide "the Master" with evidence to that effect - evidence which can be used against them later if they try to get out of line."

"It seems to me," Blake commented, "that a lot of the black magician's power is just the psychology of fear."

"Quite right," Ashton continued. "Fear, bravado - and very often sex and drugs. They start people on drug taking with the excuse that it will open up their psychic powers or some such yarn. This is a dangerous half-truth, because there are certain natural substances, known to traditional witches and shamans for centuries, which certainly will induce visions and sometimes astral projection. But this is a very secret and specialised branch of occult knowledge, well beyond the scope of dabblers like Master Nicholas. His sort are more likely to be concerned with commercial drug-pushing, just as the use of sex in their rituals is mainly for their own gratification, to establish domination over their female followers - and sometimes over their male followers too. Of the real ancient sex magic they know little or nothing. But I mustn't embark on a lecture over the telephone. What I wanted to tell you is that a critical time in the magical calendar is approaching - the night of Halloween at the end of this month of October. I am certain that Master Nicholas will try to lay on some stunt or other at that time, in order to keep his followers impressed. And if we can discover his plans, that may be how we will have him!"

"How are we going to do that?" asked Blake.

"There are some people that I want to call on," Ashton replied. "I've made an appointment to see them and I'd like you to come and meet them too. They're old acquaintances of mine, very discreet. And they'll have their own reasons for wanting to help."

Blake readily agreed and arrangements were duly made. On a bright autumn weekend, with the leaves just beginning to turn and assume their brief glory of red and gold, he drove out to Ashton's cottage. From there they continued at Ashton's direction, deep into the Sussex countryside.

They eventually arrived at an isolated small-holding in the vicinity of the little town where Henderson's shop was located. It was an old, sprawling cottage surrounded by farmland and woods, with a large kitchen-garden, an orchard and a variety of livestock which included dogs, cats, chickens, goats and bees. Blake guessed that the occupants could be almost self-sufficient, if they were contented with a simple and hardworking life.

They were welcomed in by the man they had come to see, who shared the cottage with his daughter and son-in-law. His name was George Attwood. "Old George, they generally call me," he said with a twinkle in his aged blue eyes. He had the suntanned, weather-beaten face of a working farmer; but he was evidently capable of artistry and imagination. The cottage walls were hung liberally with pictures of the old man's painting, usually depicting Sussex landscapes and the ever-changing moods of earth and sky.

The son-in-law was at work in the fields, so the daughter dispensed hospitality in the shape of plentiful cups of strong tea and home-made cake. Blake and Ashton shared the meal and watched the afternoon sun mellowing the light upon the scented herbs and late-lingering flowers in the cottage garden, while Old George talked of gardening, beekeeping and similar countryside topics.

Eventually, however, the tea-things were cleared away and the top of the ancient, well-polished table laid bare. The daughter lit the fire that was already laid in the grate and then retired to another room and left the menfolk alone to discuss the real purpose of their visit.

"I've already acquainted George with what's been happening," Ashton told Blake. "And he has some local knowledge which I think may prove very useful."

"What we want to know now," Old George remarked in his pleasant, rather deep voice with a touch of Sussex accent about it, "is what this Master Nicholas will be up to next, now that Halloween is nearly on us. There's a time-honoured way of finding things out, which our friend here knows all about. But you, Mr. Blake, may not have seen it before." His words were addressed to Blake, but then he looked enquiringly at Ashton.

"It's all right," Ashton assured him. "Jeremy and I have seen quite a few things together, though not by that particular method. I take it you mean the crystal?"

"I do," Old George answered, as he rose from his chair and went to a large carved oaken cupboard in the corner. He opened it with a key from the bunch that hung from his wide leather belt and took out various objects, which he set out upon the table. Then he drew the curtains, plunging the room into a dim twilight.

"It's nearly sunset," he remarked. "The best time."

The old man went about his preparations in an unhurried way, setting two beeswax candles into wrought iron candlesticks to enhance the flickering firelight. He placed these upon the mantelpiece, so that when, with Ashton's help, he had moved the table into the centre of the room, he could sit with their light behind him. Then he ignited a block of charcoal and placed it in a small brass incense burner of antique oriental appearance. (In fact, it was one that Ashton had procured for him). On to the glowing charcoal he sprinkled some incense from a little box. Having seen the herb-garden outside, Blake

144

guessed that the incense was home-made. It had a woody, spicy smell, quite different from the sickly sweetness of many commercially-made incenses. It made one think of deep forests in the summer heat and of secret places where fairies might haunt, upon the borderland of other realms. Indeed by, the glow of candle-light and firelight, with the rare scent of the incense filling the room, the 'borderland' feeling soon became quite strong, so that Blake and Ashton fell spontaneously silent and awaited events.

The old man invited his two guests to sit at the table on either side of him. Then he unveiled an object which he had placed before him on the table wrapped in a heavy black silk cloth. This proved to be a very large and clear crystal ball upon a wooden stand of dark oak.

There was a minimum of ceremony. The old man held both his hands over the crystal, murmuring an invocation:

"Thou Ancient Providence, who art the author of all good things, strengthen, we beseech thee, thy servants, that we may stand fast without fear throughout this dealing and work. Enlighten the dark understanding of thy creatures, so that our spiritual eye may be opened to know and see the spirits descending in this crystal. And may this shewstone or speculum be consecrated and blessed to this purpose, that no evil phantasm or deception may appear therein. By all things created and contained in the firmament and by their virtues and powers, I constrain the spirits to appear visibly in this crystal stone, in fair form and shape and without any hurt or danger of our bodies or souls and truly to inform and show unto us the visions of all things that we require, without any hindrance or tarrying, to appear visibly, by this bond of words. By the powers of the Art Magical, by the Lady of the Moon and the Lord of Death and Resurrection and by their most potent and secret names, by the spirits of the elements of life, Flatus, Ignis, Aqua, Terra, fiat, fiat, fiat!"

"So mote it be," whispered. Ashton. The three sat in silence, quietly awaiting results. The seer appeared to be in a state of deep concentration, yet relaxed rather than tense, so that this mood was communicated to the observers also.

Presently he began to speak, in a low voice as if describing a dream.

"Yes, they are there. I recognise the place. It does not belong to them but to others - we who have been there before. The woodland glade when the moon is shining. The three paths and the witches seat. The old rhyme told them:

> *At middle hour of night*
> *The full moon shineth bright.*
> *Her rays do light us well.*
> *And at the witches seat.*
> *At place where three ways meet,*
> *'Tis there we cast the spell.*

Hide in the bushes and watch them. A crowd - bringing a young girl in white. They are coming along the path, bearing a board and trestles for a table. All cloaked, except the girl in white. She has been drugged and they have to lead her. One bears a candle in a lantern, another a censer of incense. Another has a sword and the stolen thing! Yes, I see them - and I see that which pursues them! Powerful and evil - be on guard! The powers of this place are against them, they reject them - and there is also the evil spirit! Do that which you have to do, which you should have done before. But save the girl - there will be trouble and confusion. The powers of darkness have come upon the scene, swirling black clouds and the witch-ball shining in the midst. And suddenly it changes to the moon and all is calm. It is fate."

There was a pause; then the seer drew a long breath, saying, "I think that is all." He blinked and drew his hands over his face and head several times, as he returned to normal consciousness.

Blake could make very little of it and privately thought it not very helpful. But Ashton seemed quietly satisfied.

"You definitely know this place?" he asked Old George, after a few minutes rest in silence.

"Oh, yes," the old man replied. "I'll draw a little map for you later on. There's quite a bit of local folklore about it. That's probably what Master Nicholas has got hold of. That little rhyme about the Witches Seat - it's quite well-known to the older generation around here."

He laughed rather ruefully. "That's the trouble with these old places. They get known and then we can't use them any more, or at least not on the dates everybody knows such as May Eve or Halloween. Like Chanctonbury Ring these days - and Pendle Hill too, I'm told."

"And this Witches Seat?" Ashton queried. "What is it?"

"It's the usual thing," came the answer. "An old tree curiously twisted so that the branches make a sort of natural throne. You know how they sometimes make one out of a suitable tree, by lopping out the central trunk and letting five thick branches grow up round it; but this one is formed naturally and very old, so it's more powerful. It's just in the right place, too, where three paths meet and form a clearing. So you can imagine it's been well used. And now these people have got it; but not for long, I think."

A suspicion stirred in Blake's mind as to the possible identity of his hosts. Was this remote cottage and its inhabitants a secret stronghold of that which its followers called the Old Religion - witchcraft?

There was nothing sinister in the atmosphere, but certainly something strange. Old George with his herb-garden and his bees; his daughter, dark-haired and rosy-cheeked, amiable but not talkative. The son-in-law, evidently a hard-working farmer. And he understood from previous conversation that there were several grandchildren around the countryside. A normal enough family, if you excepted Old George's powers of clairvoyance. Yet the way that little séance had been conducted was very different from the sort of amateur Spiritualism that was popular with middle-class ladies. It was more like something from the Middle Ages. Moreover, Old George had been very practiced and confident, yet neither was he in the least like a slick professional who worked for a fee. Blake wondered; but kept his wondering to himself for the time being.

Old George rose and carefully re-wrapped the crystal, before lighting a shaded table-lamp. He extinguished the candles and the incense, saying:

"Thanks be to the Powers. May all spirits who have been attracted by this ritual now be released and may there be peace between us and them. Hail and farewell!"

He carefully replaced everything within the cupboard and locked it up. Then he produced from the sideboard a bottle of home-made mead and some wine-glasses. Blake got the impression that sharing this drink was somehow part of the ritual, a kind of unwinding of tension by all concerned.

So he gratefully accepted his wine-glass and found its contents subtly flavoured and delicious. He permitted Old George, now completely returned to everyday normality, to replenish the glass; but Ashton, who knew the strength of Old George's brew, politely declined a second drink as he was driving.

They left in a cheerful mood, with laughter and promises to come again. But as they drove back in the dark to Ashton's home, the warm glow of the mead eventually wore off and left Blake rather puzzled.

"Your friends are interesting people," he remarked to Ashton. "But I don't quite see how we're much forwarder."

"*Charming* people is a good way to describe them," said Ashton with a laugh. "I expect you have guessed why - and just what their special reasons might be for wanting to help in this affair. But don't you see? Now we know what to do. Old George sketched me out that little map while you were out of the room and I'll check it with the Ordnance Map when we get home. I've a good idea where the place is, so on Halloween we'll do what Old George said - hide in the bushes and wait for them. It'll be nearly full moon this year on that night; I've already checked on it, so we'll have some light."

"But we can't take on that crowd," Blake objected. "You'd better let me bring in those two pals of mine I told you about. And even then we'll be outnumbered if it comes to a punch-up."

"No, I don't think so," Ashton answered after a moment's thought. "It's my impression that the trouble is going to be psychic rather than physical. And in that event your muscular friends might panic and be more hindrance than help. I think we should just watch and wait, but be prepared to act when the opportunity arises. Well, we're nearly home - to my place, anyway. Come in and have a bite to eat before you go back to Brighton."

They laid plans for Halloween accordingly, over supper at Ashton's cottage. Blake was not entirely happy with them; but he had learned from experience to trust Ashton's judgment, so he acquiesced.

The last day of October duly arrived; Halloween, Hollantide, Spunky Night, Mischief Night, or Samhain Eve, according to where in the British Isles one lived. For once, the autumn gales had given the land a few days respite and the weather was fine and clear with just a hint of frost. The time had come for Blake and Ashton to put their plans into practice. A previous reconnoitre of the traditional witches meeting place in the woodland had been carried out in daylight, in order to settle such mundane matters as discreet car-parking and the best place for observers to hide. Conversation at the local pub had acquainted them with the fact that the woodland they were interested in bore a vaguely sinister reputation of being haunted, though no one seemed to know exactly why.

"I'm not surprised at this story," Ashton told Blake. "This is a typical ploy of the old-time witches, to spread ghostly yarns about places they wanted to use for meetings, in order to scare people away. Sometimes they would even dress up in ragged clothes and masks and stage something that would grow into a local legend. Smugglers used to do the same. Of course, people were more credulous in the olden days. Today, they would be more likely to bring a crowd of psychical researchers down on them by doing things like that!"

"There *is* a strange feeling about that wood, though", remarked Blake. "I noticed that some of the trees looked pretty old. It could even be part of the old Andredsweald, the great forest that used to stretch right across southern England from Kent to Hampshire. A lot of these odd pockets of Sussex woodland are." He had begun to take more interest in such things since he had known Ashton.

"Yes, I noticed it," Ashton responded. "But there is always latent power in woodland. Trees have auras, you know, the same as people. I could tell you many things about that. But we'd better get a move on if we want to take up our positions before moonrise. I fixed up yesterday with the landlord of the pub to leave the car in his car park. I told him we were going to a party locally and paid my footing by buying several bottles of drink off him. This means that we'll have to walk to the wood; but I don't want Master Nicholas and his friends to see our car parked anywhere around there or they might get suspicious."

They had already agreed to use Ashton's car as being older and less conspicuous than Blake's; and they set off accordingly from Ashton's cottage as dusk was approaching.

The night was mild and lit by the evening star as they arrived at the pub car park. The last glow of sunset still lingered in the west and there was a chattering of birds in the surrounding trees. They locked the car and left it well out of the way in the car-park, then set out on the walk to the wood. It was dark by the time they arrived, but they ventured to use the light of small electric torches to find their way to the place they had selected for a suitable hide. This looked on to the clearing formed by the junction of the three footpaths and gave them a good view of the tree called the Witches Seat.

"We may be in for a long wait," Ashton whispered to Blake, "but I couldn't risk them getting here before us. Anyway, we've got this groundsheet to sit on. And the longer we stay here quietly, the more our eyes will get used to the darkness and our ears become alert for any sound."

Both men were warmly dressed in duffle coats and thick boots. In addition to this physical protection, Ashton had hung around his neck upon a silver chain an amulet consisting of a heavy silver disc engraved with a five-pointed star upon one side and a six-pointed star upon the other, together with various Hebrew letters which spelled magical words of power. He had given a similar amulet to Blake and made sure that the younger man was wearing it.

The waiting was indeed tedious at first, until the moon rose in bright silver splendour over the trees. Then the magical transformation of moonlight spread itself through the wood, until one could even see the patterns of lichen upon the old branches. Here and there a star shone through the treetops and the wood seemed to come alive with the rustlings of small creatures in the undergrowth. An elfin feeling seemed abroad, so that it would hardly have been surprising if each large toadstool had suddenly found a goblin as its occupant, or a ring of tiny dancing fays had appeared in the midst of the clearing.

Blake commented on this in a low voice. "Be careful," Ashton whispered. "What you are becoming aware of is the build-up of elemental forces, on this night especially. Remember it is the night of one of the Great Sabbats. Listen! I think I heard a noise in the distance."

Both men kept silent and listened intently. Yes, there was definitely someone approaching. Footsteps and murmuring voices were coming through the trees. A few flashes of light became visible. It sounded as if there was a fair-sized party of people on the way towards them. Blake remembered uncomfortably the savage beating that had been administered to Henderson and needed no further admonition from Ashton to keep perfectly still and quiet.

The party came into view as they filed into the clearing. There were about a dozen of them, all dressed in cloaks or kaftans. Some of them seemed to be carrying various articles, notably a board and two trestles to form a table. There was also a swinging censer of incense, the tang of which drifted towards the two men concealed in the bushes. Other members of the group carried patio lanterns with candles in them. There was a flash of light reflected from something as the black-cloaked figure who seemed to be the leader of the party held up his arm. Blake saw that it was a short, bright-bladed sword.

But his attention was focused mainly upon one figure of the group, a young girl who was being led along by two men. She was dressed in a long white robe and seemed by the way she moved to be semi-conscious, possibly drugged. He saw her face in the moonlight, young and pretty, with fair hair that hung long and loose down her back. In a sudden flash of memory, he recalled the words of the seer, the old man who had gazed into the crystal. Hadn't he described this scene exactly? The girl in white - the men bearing the trestle table - the sword - the censer of incense - yes, it was all here. But where was 'the stolen thing'? And how were they going to carry out Old George's injunction to 'save the girl'?

Then as the table, evidently an improvised altar, was erected, Blake saw the finishing touch to the re-enactment of the old man's vision. A black cloth with a design of a five-pointed star upon it was spread upon the table and in the centre of it, with a flourish, the leader placed an object he had produced from a bag. The missing witch-ball!

Candles in lanterns were soon displayed on either side of the witch-ball, while the incense in the censer was replenished by the tall, thin man who carried it and who seemed to be older than the rest. The man with the sword, whom they guessed to be Master Nicholas, called his followers together and proceeded to draw around them and the altar a large circle, using the sword to do so. He was followed by the other man with the swinging censer.

Standing before the altar and facing his congregation, Master Nicholas flung up his arms dramatically and cried, "Hail Satan-Lucifer! Hail Ashtoreth!" All the others present repeated the words in response. This was done three times. Then Nicholas lowered his arms and stepped aside to make room for the tall man who had borne the censer.

This man now placed the censer of incense upon the altar and raising his arms began a long chant. It seemed to be in Latin, but Blake could not at first make out the significance of it:

*"Malo a nos libera sed. Tentationem in inducas nos*
*ne et. Nostris debitoribus dimittimus nos et sicut.*
*Nostra debits nobis dimitte et. Hodie nobis da quotidianum*
*nostrum panem. Terra in et caelo in sicut, tua voluntas*
*fiat. Tuum regnum adveniat. Tuum nomen sanctificetur. Caelis in es*
*qui, noster pater."*

All the congregation responded with cries of *"Nema! Nema! Nema!"* Then Blake realised what the chant had been; the Lord's Prayer in Latin - but backwards.

The cries of the assembled worshippers became shrill, almost hysterical. Hand in hand, they began to dance wildly around the circle, dragging the white-robed girl with them. Under cover of the noise, Ashton whispered to Blake, "I know who that fellow is who did the chanting; a renegade priest. This crowd are more literate than I thought."

Blake shivered. Suddenly the moonlit wood had become sinister and evil. The atmosphere of the place was changing, as if not elves but demons lurked in the shadows. Another chant had been taken up, slower, more deliberate, accompanied by hand-clapping as the circling dance progressed:

*"Emen-hetan! Emen-hetan!*
*Ee-oh! Ee-oh! Hoo-hoo-hoo!*
*Emen-hetan! Emen-hetan!*
*Ee-oh! Ee-oh! Hoo-hoo-hoo!"*

It was repeated again and again, rhythmically, hypnotically, until it began to have the same effect as voodoo drums. The white-robed girl sank to the ground in front of the altar and began to roll about convulsively, laughing and sobbing. Blake could see her quite clearly through the gaps between the robed figures as they passed and repassed. Why *could* he see her so clearly? What was happening?

He gripped Ashton's arm. "That light! Look - look at the *witch-ball!*"

"Hush," Ashton whispered in response, "it is a cone of power forming over the altar. The witch-ball is the centre of it. Keep calm and watch!"

A strange green light was glowing over the altar, rising up in a vague cone-shape, or like the shining aura depicted around gods and spirits in Tibetan paintings, except that there was nothing celestial about this manifestation. Its colour was baleful and eerie. The wood had become chill and there was a tension of terror in the air.

At first, Master Nicholas and his followers did not seem to have noticed the manifestation, intent as they were upon dancing and chanting. Then they did! There were the sounds of feminine screams, as several of the robed figures tried to run away and were restrained forcibly by others. Master Nicholas tried to rally his frightened followers by crying out an invocation as the dance showed signs of breaking up in confusion:

*"Hail Satan! Hail Ashtoreth! Hail..."*

His voice, already shaking, trailed off into a terrified squeal as the light above the altar grew denser and in the midst of it a fiendish face began to form. Blake, watching from the shadows, gasped; but Ashton remained steady as a rock, for he had seen that face before.

It was the face of a woman, beautiful but indescribably evil and menacing, Gorgon-like, surrounded by black flowing ringlets of hair. The glittering dark eyes turned themselves to glare at Master Nicholas and the red lips parted in a cruel, mirthless smile.

At that moment, the girl who had been writhing on the ground before the altar, staining her white robe with earth and fallen leaves, leaped up shrieking, "Murder! Death! I am the spirit of murder!"

She continued waving her arms and babbling incoherently as the crowd broke up in panic fear and fairly took to their heels down the path. As they passed Blake and Ashton's hideout, it was apparent that no one was running harder or looking more terrified than the erstwhile 'Master', Nicholas Dee!

Ashton shook off Blake's grip and urged him into movement, saying, "*Now*, Blake, quickly! I'll grab the witch-ball and you grab the girl!"

With the break-up of the circle the eldritch light had faded and the face disappeared. But Blake noticed that as Ashton dashed towards the altar he pulled open his coat so that the shining amulet he wore about his neck plainly confronted anything that was there. Blake did the same, then ran towards the girl and seized her in his arms.

She struggled briefly, glaring at him with a look horribly reminiscent of the apparition. Then she suddenly went limp; the hideous look faded as she slumped unconscious and he had to lift and carry her.

"What now?" he asked Ashton.

"We've got to get out of here, before that lot has a chance to collect their wits," Ashton replied. "There's another way out of the woods this way. Follow me down this path."

Their roundabout route back to the car was difficult, with only the moonlight to help them at first. When they had got a suitable distance to venture to use a light, they stopped to bring the girl round and reassure her that she was in safe hands. Blake took off his duffle coat and wrapped her in it, comforting her as she began to cry. She was wearing nothing on her feet but light sandals, so he continued to carry her as they proceeded on their way. Ashton noted that he seemed very willing to do so and wondered for a moment about the old seer's words, "Save the girl......... It is fate."

They decided to tell anyone who questioned them that 'the young lady had had a few drinks and they were taking her home'. Fortunately, however, they saw no one as they reached the pub car park and hastily got into Ashton's car and drove off, Blake sitting in the back with the girl as Ashton took the wheel. Beside him on the front passenger seat reposed his prize of the night, the gleaming witch-ball; but he paid it no attention and kept his eyes firmly on the road.

It was about a week later when Blake and Ashton again foregathered in the firelit comfort of Ashton's cottage. With them was the young girl Blake had carried off from the black coven's Halloween meeting. Her name proved to be Janet MacGregor, an office worker for a large company in Brighton. She was intelligent and well-educated as well as being pretty, which caused Ashton to wonder how she had come to be involved with a dubious character like Master Nicholas.

"I have always been interested in the occult," she told him. "I know there is something in it because I have had psychic experiences of my own. You know, true dreams, hunches, premonitions, all that sort of thing. My great-grandmother in the Scottish Highlands was supposed to be a witch."

She laughed rather nervously as she accepted the cup of tea and plate of toasted tea-cakes that Blake attentively handed her.

"I see," said Ashton with a smile. "No wonder Master Nicholas wanted you. You are a natural psychic. Yes, that explains several things. I suppose he promised you all sorts of marvellous developments, too?"

"Yes, if I would consent to be initiated. It was to be done that night." Janet seemed rather embarrassed as she answered.

"It's all right. I can guess what that was going to involve," said Ashton gently. "Bogus magicians like Master Nicholas usually demand sexual submission of some kind from their followers.

In fact, you might call this sort of demand one of their trademarks."

"Was I wrong to want to develop my gifts?" Janet asked.

"No, of course not," Ashton responded. "Gifts like yours are natural. In fact, I believe they are latent in everyone. Consequently, it is worse than useless to be afraid of them. But there are wise and unwise ways of going about such development. If you will allow me to advise you, I may be able to help you. That is, if Jeremy has no objection to your joining our friendship?" He looked quizzically at Blake as he spoke, being well able to see that nothing would please that young man better.

"Jeremy's been very kind," Janet broke in, as Blake uttered some confused words of acceptance. "In fact, I don't know how I would have got over that ghastly experience if it hadn't been for him. I still don't quite understand what happened."

"Well," said Ashton, "let's start with the fact that it was Halloween. This is the ancient Celtic feast of the dead, Christianised by the Church into the Eve of All Hallows or All Saints. It is one of the four Great Sabbats of the witches, the followers of the old religion of nature-worship that is the remainder of the primordial faith of Western Europe - the genuine witches, that is, not phonies like Master Nicholas. It is a night of power; and Master Nicholas, having that little knowledge which is proverbially a dangerous thing, wanted to use that power.

"Now, that place he took you to is a traditional meeting place of the witches. That strange old tree called the Witches Seat is where the High Priestess used to sit, when the coven danced around her and invoked the spirits of those who had been great witches of the past to come and speak through her entranced lips, upon this night of all nights when the dead could communicate with the living. But because Master Nicholas was a usurper there, an interloper where he had no right to be, the entity which manifested was hostile and dangerous. In fact, it was the evil, earth-bound spirit attached to that stolen witch-ball. I expect Jeremy has told you the history of that thing? Well, just for a while that spirit tried to take you over. But don't worry." (He had seen a look of fear pass across Janet's face).

"The witch-ball will do no more harm. I have done now what I should have done before - subjected it to a thorough ceremony of exorcism and banishing. Afterwards, I took it back to Henderson's shop; but he and his wife were unanimous that they never wanted to see the thing again, so I'm keeping it in my collection. I'll probably hang it up somewhere, it's quite a handsome piece.

"I don't think Master Nicholas will do much more harm, either. Not for a while, anyway, for two reasons. The first one is that after his followers have seen him lose his nerve and run like a rabbit, he's not going to have much influence over them again."

Ashton chuckled at the recollection. "You know, there's nothing like a bit of *real* occult phenomena to put the wind up the pretenders. I've seen it happen many times."

Blake gave a shudder, in spite of the cheerful surroundings of Ashton's familiar fireside and the comfortable hospitality of the meal.

"I don't mind telling you," he remarked, "that that manifestation put the wind up me, too. It will be a long time before I can forget that phantom face and the dreadful look upon it."

"The spirit has been helped upon its way," said Ashton with quiet seriousness. "It will trouble us no more. But I must tell you the other reason why I think Master Nicholas will not be bothering us, either. It seems that he and his crowd had arrived the other night at the woods in an old van. Well, when they all came running back down the path in a state of panic, they piled into this van and drove off so erratically and at such a speed that they ended up in a ditch. A police car came by and stopped to investigate the accident. No one was hurt, but as you can imagine the account they gave of themselves was pretty incoherent and the officers became suspicious. They checked on the van's registration number and found it was on the list of stolen vehicles. My local journalist friend told me this and it sounds as if Master Nicholas will have quite a few other charges to answer, too; dangerous driving, no valid licence, no insurance - I think he's got enough on his plate to keep him out of mischief for a while."

Blake laughed aloud. "Can you picture it? The great and terrible High Priest of Satan being hauled up before the beak for dangerous driving in a tatty old van! It reminds me of Al Capone being done for tax evasion."

He finished off the toasted tea-cakes with relish as Janet in turn laughed at the recollection of the man she had once feared.

Ashton looked benignly at the two of them together. If he was not mistaken, they would make a very nice young couple. And in the future, perhaps, Janet would join Blake and himself in the eternal quest for the age-old knowledge and wisdom to be found in the mysterious realms of the occult.

THE END.

## The Doreen Valiente Foundation & The Centre For Pagan Studies

The Doreen Valiente Foundation is a charitable trust dedicated to the protection and preservation of material relating to Pagan practices, spirituality and religion. The Foundation is also dedicated to researching and interpreting this material and making such research and the material itself accessible to the public for the benefit of wider education and the advancement of knowledge in this unique landscape of living cultural and religious heritage.

The Foundation was established in 2011 and received legal ownership of Doreen Valiente's entire legacy of artefacts, books, writings, documents, manuscripts and copyrights under a deed of trust that permanently prevents the sale or splitting up of the collection and prohibits the making of profit through exploitation of the collection. This means that every penny earned by the Foundation (including the publishers' proceeds of the sale of this book) is spent on pursuing its goals and charitable objects as above.

The Foundation runs a number of ongoing projects, working towards the establishment of a permanent museum home for the collection and the physical creation of a Centre For Pagan Studies which is the organisation of which Doreen was patron shortly before her death in 1999. The Foundation succeeded in campaigns to have Heritage Blue Plaques placed on the former homes of Doreen Valiente and Gerald Gardner with others to follow. The DVF and CFPS also organises conferences, talks and exhibitions as well as engaging with the global community in matters of religious history and spirtual heritage.

More information about Doreen Valiente, The Doreen Valiente Foundation and The Centre For Pagan Studies, including foundation membership, details of events and activities, purchase of Doreen Valiente merchandise, books etc and donations can be found at:

**www.doreenvaliente.org**
and
**www.centre-for-pagan-studies.com**